STRETCHING
THEIR BODIES

STRETCHING
THEIR BODIES

The History of Physical Education

W. David Smith

DAVID & CHARLES

NEWTON ABBOT LONDON
NORTH POMFRET (VT) VANCOUVER

0 7153 6341 7

Set in 11 on 13pt Garamond and printed in
Great Britain by Latimer Trend & Company Ltd
for David & Charles (Holdings) Limited
South Devon House Newton Abbot Devon

Published in the United States of America
by David & Charles Inc North Pomfret
Vermont 05053 USA

Published in Canada by Douglas David &
Charles Limited 3645 McKechnie Drive
West Vancouver BC

74 8712

Contents

TO MALI AND DEBORAH

I

Games, reform and athleticism in the public schools

They ought never to play. But they do, every day; yea in the school.
John Wesley quoted in *Three Old Boys,*
A History of Kingswood School, Bath

I have no doubt this power of getting to the inner boy life, and their trust in one in matters of this sort, is more potent for real good here than all the rest of my work almost put together.
Edward Thring on being asked to resolve a conflict in the Games Committee, quoted in G. R. Parkin, *Edward Thring*

The sports and pastimes of the English are developed from the recreations of their ancient forebears. Primitive versions of ball games existed as early as Anglo-Saxon times, though derivative pastimes flourished or languished from time to time. In the eighteenth century football, a barbarous mass struggle played in the streets of a town or between neighbouring villages, declined, because its associated damage and disorder led to the imposition of a ban by the authorities. But in the same century cricket developed as the first popular game to be played by accepted rules. It was natural that boys should play their indigenous games at school, indeed in many instances the founders of the public schools had made provision in the statutes of the schools for the boys' recreation—encouraging especially archery, for its contribution to the defence of the realm, and sometimes discouraging the cruder activities enjoyed by the populace.[1]

7

The recreations of the boys at school were a selection of those popular in society at large, as various contemporary records show. The traditional English games developed slowly, but by the 1740s rowing and cricket were established at Westminster and by the 1760s cricket was popular at Harrow.[2] By the end of the century this game was played in the other older public schools, while there were similar developments in team games in many of the private academies.[3] The public schools, however, were distinguished by the boys' freedom, claimed as an established right, from supervision outside the classroom. This freedom of the boys to organise their own society and to conduct their own lives was an aspect of the accepted function of the schools, which was to develop character rather than to impart useful knowledge or to develop social attitudes or Christian attributes. Being left to organise and develop games was thus a part of tradition, other aspects of which were fagging, slang, dress and breaking bounds. The bullying and toughness which were an integral part of the boys' direction of their own affairs were regarded as essential for the development of leadership, courage and stamina.

To defend rights and usages established by tradition the boys were willing to go to any lengths, even to rebellion against the school authorities. The first revolt at Eton occurred in 1768; during the next seventy years each great school had at least one major rebellion. Even so renowned a flogger as Dr Keate faced three major uprisings during his reign at Eton between 1809 and 1834. The last, which occurred near his retirement, was the result of the imposition of roll-calls interfering with the established convivialities of boat crews on Saturday nights. On this occasion Keate flogged almost eighty boys![4] It is evident that freedom to retain choice of recreation was a carefully guarded prerogative.

The character-training undertaken by the schools was rigorously planned. The scheme of studies, based on the classics, provided an excellent base because the classics were difficult; the maintenance of discipline was by ubiquitous flogging; primitive living conditions and bad food contributed to an environment in

8

which grit and stamina were required for survival. Brutality was encouraged both by the primitive living conditions and by the severity of the punishments inflicted by masters. It is not surprising that where the boys themselves possessed authority it led to the slavery of fagging and such bullying as the 'initiation' of new boys and 'roastings'. The result was a barbarous society: described by Lytton Strachey as 'a system of anarchy tempered by despotism . . . a life in which licensed barbarism was mingled with the daily and hourly study of the niceties of Ovidian verse'.[5] Certainly the 'wild profligacy' of the Long Chamber at Eton (a large dormitory where the boys were locked in at night) and the battling fury of the Westminster boys gave the schools an unenviable reputation.

The special contribution of the public schools to physical education was in the development of ball games, from their crude beginnings into games with definite rules and penalties. Organised football was a product of the nineteenth century: initially each school had its own version, some of them highly idiosyncratic. Numbers of players were unrestricted for many years, while contests were long drawn out and fierce. It may well be imagined that the first picking up and running with the ball, which became the distinguishing feature of the Rugby game, was the result of frustration from playing in a seething mass of bodies. Another example of the irrelevance of rules is seen in the characteristic feature of the Winchester game known as a 'hot'—a free-for-all ungoverned by any restriction.

Sport was regarded by the masters as an activity to be organised by the boys, for none of them yet regarded games in themselves as a means of character training. The attitude of individual headmasters ranged from intense hostility—such as that of Dr Heath who had forbidden the first inter-school cricket match between Westminster and Eton in 1796 and who had flogged the entire Eton eleven when his authority was flouted—to tolerance and even support by the provision of facilities. Dr Goodall patronised the Eton–MCC fixture in 1808,[6] while in the same year Dean Vincent preserved ten acres of Toothill Fields for the use of the boys of Westminster School, on the occasion of the enclosure of what had been for centuries their traditional playground.[7] At Shrewsbury, Dr Samuel Butler, headmaster from 1798 to 1836, had accepted cricket but forbidden boating and football. The staff at Harrow seem to have been encouraging games as early as the 1820s according to Charles Wordsworth, the boys even hiring a cricket professional to coach them for their match against Eton. The effect of personal example and influence was seen when Wordsworth became second master at Winchester in 1835, for his appointment presaged the swift rise of the school to prominence in cricket. B. H. Kennedy, on the other hand, was determined to keep games in their place when he was appointed to succeed Butler at Shrewsbury in 1836; as an assistant master at Harrow he had considered cricket and football 'so zealously pursued and with such organisation of the whole school that it is vain to expect anything like extensive reading and sound scholarship'.[8]

Some form of cricket or football, athletics and cross-country running were universal features by 1840, part of a vast array of sports such as boating, boxing, single-stick, swimming, fives, racquets and quoits. Certain schools with access to a river developed rowing as a speciality; others had particular interests in race meetings and hunting. The fact that the boys were not wholly concerned with the developing team games can be seen from the persistence of traditional seasonal games such as tops, hopscotch and marbles, and by the retention of the cherished right to wander in the local countryside.

THE REFORM OF THE PUBLIC SCHOOLS

There were many pressures upon the public schools to make them introduce reforms, though their continuing commercial viability was the one which most concerned the school authorities; for the schools were subject to wide fluctuations in their total size and in their entries, and consequently in their prosperity. The entry at Shrewsbury varied between 9 in 1807 and 104 in 1826; Harrow declined from 295 in 1816 to 128 in 1828 and to 69 in 1844, and Rugby fell from 300 in 1821 to 123 when Arnold was appointed in 1827.[9] Each school had a unique record of fluctuation, though there was a general pattern of decline until enlightened headmasters undertook the broadening of the curriculum and the removal of the disorder and brutality associated with school life. Middle-class pressure worked for such changes. The demand for education was accentuated by the growth of the population, and especially of the professional classes in the rapidly expanding towns. The ambitious fathers of this section of the population saw education as fulfilling their aspirations both for the careers of their sons and for their social advancement, however unrealistic this view might have been.[10] But middle-class patronage of the schools was conditional upon their reform. If this were to be accomplished it had, in the main, to be the work of individuals: significantly Russell, Samuel Butler and Thomas Arnold were not fettered by collegiate ecclesiastical organisation and were at schools patronised by the middle class.

It was Arnold who made the main contribution to the sweeping reform of moral tone. Deeply impressed by the innate sinfulness of boys, he wished to create an environment in which they would learn quickly to abandon their childishness and selfishness, acquiring instead a deeply-rooted sense of moral rectitude. He did not wish to change the traditions of the public school but to adapt them to his own purpose. He placed greatest reliance on the leadership and example of his senior boys, exalting the status of the sixth form by the reinforcement of traditional disciplinary powers. He was the first headmaster who also became the chaplain wishing to inspire boys with a new religious spirit, and he sought, by befriending his boys, especially the seniors, to end the traditional notion of the 'natural enmity' of boys and masters. Arnold still flogged boys; he still used the classics as the medium of instruction (though, as he saw the chief revelation of God to be in history, he stressed the historical and philosophical content of the works rather than their style), and he maintained the traditional freedom of the boys. To him, 'a school was a testing place of virtue, and untried goodness was worthless'.

Whether or not Arnold has deserved his reputation as the great reformer of the public schools has long been a subject of controversy; however, the extent and lasting nature of his influence is undoubted. His work was copied immediately in those schools established to meet growing middle-class demands, for Rugby School became a nursery for headmasters. The general adoption of the Rugby game is an indication of the spread of his methods. The main criticisms of Arnold's work have been firstly that he exerted too much moral pressure upon boys and loaded many of them with responsibility before they were sufficiently mature to carry it; secondly, that by stressing moral qualities he denigrated intelligence; thirdly, that by giving greatly increased power to prefects he created the conditions in which 'athleticism' flourished:

> The earnest enthusiast who strove to make his pupils Christian gentlemen and who governed his school according to the principles of the Old Testament has proved to be the founder of the worship of athletics and the worship of good form. Upon those two poles our public schools have thrived for so long that we have almost come to believe that such is their essential nature, and that an English public schoolboy who wears the wrong clothes and takes no interest in football is a contradiction in terms.[11]

Arnold's view of the place of physical activities in school life seems clear. He took a personal delight in exercise, writing of his games with the boys he taught at the private school at Laleham.[12] One of his fears when going to Rugby was that he would be denied the opportunity of personal physical relaxation, so to ensure his daily exercise, in 1831 he erected an apparatus called a 'gallows'. He was influenced by the writings of Francis Lieber, the tutor of Niebuhr's children and fervent disciple of Jahn, the great German gymnast.[13] It seems evident that his personal interest and participation in daily exercise stimulated emulation amongst the boys. Games developed so rapidly at Rugby during Arnold's time, that Queen Adelaide asked to watch a football match during her visit to the school in 1839, and the eleven played their first cricket match at Lord's in 1840.[14] Yet there is no evidence that Arnold believed that games served any purpose other than to provide healthy means of satisfying their need of exercise and their exuberance; there is nothing to indicate that he believed games to be of any significance in the development of character, which was the essential basis for their later development in schools. Arnold was clearly influenced by disciplinary considerations, being determined to end the abuses associated with trespassing, poaching and drunkenness. He considered clearly that the physical aspect of education played a subordinate role to that of intellectual and moral considerations, writing of the educator's function to 'consider every part of his pupil's nature, physical, intellectual and moral; regarding the cultivation of the last, however, as paramount to either of the others'.[15]

The difference between Arnold's idealism and the philosophy of the Muscular Christians who claimed him as their inspiration is demonstrable. Arnold's belief that all the powers given to man were intended to be developed to their utmost in the fulfilment of God's purpose implied a new appreciation of the value of physical recreation and the abandonment of previously held attitudes. In his sermon 'On Christian Education' he examines the problem of reconciling 'with a profession of religious or Christian education, the devotion of so much time to studies not supposed to be religious'; he continues:

> Undoubtedly that is useless in education, which does not enable man to glorify God better in his way through life; but then we are called upon to glorify him in many various ways . . . I cannot consider it unworthy either to render our body strong and active, or our understanding clear, rich and versatile in its powers: I cannot reject from the range of religious education whatever ministers to our bodies and our minds, so long as both in body and mind, in soul and spirit, we ourselves may be taught to minister to the service of God.[16]

It is evidently only a small step from this standpoint to seeing the justification of the pursuit of physical activities as for a moral purpose.

Arnold's idealism must also be viewed in the context of changing patterns of recreation in society. William Howitt wrote joyfully in 1838 of the 'mighty revolution' in the sports and pastimes of the common people in rural society, welcoming the decline of brutal sports and the revival of interest in activities reflecting the development of a greater humanity and decency in social intercourse. Despite the dire predictions that the loss of brutal sports would lead to a decline in the fighting spirit of the Englishman, middle-class abhorrence of the barbarity and cruelty involved triumphed, the prohibition of cockfighting in 1835 being the last official sanction.[17]

The moral benefits associated with the development of sport were also apparent; Howitt writes of the crowd at a cricket match:

> What a wide difference was here presented, to the rude rabbles formerly assembled to the most barbarous and blackguard amusements imaginable . . . twenty thousand people can now sit, day after day, to witness a contest of manly activity and pure skill, and enjoy a high delight without drunkenness and brutal rows.

A contemporary writer quoting Dr Arnold as authority for the opinion that intellectual attainment is of little value compared with 'moral knowledge of right and wrong', advocated the development of humanising pastimes and concluded:

> It is among the truths of every day's experience, that it is one of the greatest errors to decry amusements not of an intellectual cast. The game at cricket, the exercise at fencing, or other manual sports or social meeting, will dissipate a fit of spleen, which the whole order of book idolaters, savons and philosophers must turn away so irremediable.[18]

The dilution and misinterpretation of Arnold's 'manly piety' was further encouraged by the publication in 1857 and later success of *Tom Brown's Schooldays*. The portrait of Arnold in the book is an idealisation of one whose greatest achievements in his schooldays had been in football and cricket. Hughes had not known the friendly intimacy with Arnold which his biographer A. P. Stanley had enjoyed as a boy; significantly, Stanley found in the book a revelation of a world he had not known at school. Hughes's concern is didactic but he is also essentially anti-intellectual. Old Brooke's statement, 'I know I'd sooner win two School-house matches running than get the Balliol Scholarship any day' epitomises his sense of values. To Hughes the glory of organised games was their value as a medium for the creation of courageous Christian English gentlemen. To him they were the evident means of achieving Arnold's aims. The influence of the book may be seen in its wide imitation in subsequent literature and in its effect on the schools themselves. Mack and Armytage believe its influence to be of paramount importance:

> It is no exaggeration to say that *Tom Brown's Schooldays* made the modern public school. Dr Arnold had done the work of reform, bringing the eighteenth-century school into conformity with middle-class ideas of morality, humanity, discipline and learning. But Hughes's novel through its immense popularity, spread Arnold's fame abroad in a way that neither Arnold nor Stanley could spread it.[19]

This judgement cannot be accepted as it stands. Arnold's work must be seen as part of a wider movement for reform. In some ways, such as in Russell's reliance upon senior boys at Charterhouse, his work had been anticipated elsewhere, while contemporaneously Butler and Kennedy at Shrewsbury, Charles Wordsworth and Moberly at Winchester, John Hawtry at Eton, were amongst those earnestly attempting to reform the primitive conditions and low standards of the schools. There were many facets to the reform of the public schools: an improved moral tone with the raising of the status of the chapel; a discipline dependent upon boy-authority in the prefectorial system; the broadening of the curriculum to include mathematics and French; more efficient teaching to smaller classes; and the improvement of diet and housing by the establishment of housemasters. At

Eton, notoriously resistant to outside influence, the sheet-anchor of the programme of reform was the opening of the New Buildings in 1846 and the end of those dreaded dormitories, the Long Chamber and Carter's Chamber.[20]

Another qualification of Mack and Armytage's judgement quoted above must be that games at schools other than Rugby during the years before the publication of *Tom Brown's Schooldays* in 1857 had the approval and tacit or overt encouragement of the school authorities. The development of rowing at Eton illustrates this, for early races had taken place in the face of the stern opposition of headmasters who deprecated the associated publicity and beer drinking. Because the boys' boating was illegal there were no safety precautions and a number of fatal accidents. Such an occurrence in 1840 resulted in the presentation of a petition that strict safety precautions be adopted and enforced. Dr Hawtry put in his first formal appearance at a boat race in 1847. From 1850 onwards there appears to have been a more general attitude of acceptance of the place of games in school life. Their protagonists were not limited to the great public schools. At Mill Hill, founded as a Protestant Dissenters' Grammar School in 1807, where games were unorganised crude affairs, without master-participation, in the 1840s, the school secretary, the Reverend Algernon Wells, on the Speech Day of 1845 made an eloquent plea for games, 'which if not the full half of education, are still an essential part of it. They are not merely physical training, but partake of the nature of a moral discipline'.[21]

In the same decade cricket was firmly established at Uppingham, a small country grammar school, where a playing field had been rented from 1827, the lists of the elevens date from 1841 and the first old boy played for Cambridge University in 1845.[22] At Liverpool College, opened in 1843, the boys hired a cricket ground and financed the building of fives courts. Here the initiative clearly came from the boys themselves, but masters and governors were later willing to help, the latter making a grant in 1856.[23] These examples could doubtless be multiplied.

Official approval of the developing games inevitably led by a very short step to master-participation. This first took place in the rising schools, that is the grammar schools with ambition and in those schools newly founded on the model of the public schools. The 1840s and 1850s were the great decades for such establishments. A leading figure in this movement was Edward Thring, who became headmaster of Uppingham in 1853. A courageous and accomplished games player as a boy at Eton, Thring stressed the value of games at Uppingham, aiming to provide a high standard of facilities. He set a vigorous personal example in football, fives and cricket, and he and his deputy played regularly in the eleven. From 1857 onwards the Old Boys match, a two-day affair, was a regular feature.[24] To Thring, games were an essential and vital part of school life, but at Marlborough disciplinary motives for the sponsorship of games were pre-eminent. Intended to provide cheaper boarding education for the sons of clergymen, this school opened with 200 boys and soon grew to 500. There were no prefects, the boys organised no games, and gang rivalry and poaching were the chief diversions. In 1851 there was open rebellion, as the result of which G. E. L. Cotton, the 'young master' of *Tom Brown's Schooldays*, was appointed headmaster. Cotton imposed the rule of prefects, but also deliberately used games as an outlet for the boys' physical energies. So vigorous was the sponsorship of games that inter-school cricket matches were begun, with Rugby in 1855 and with Cheltenham in the following year. It seems that the effect of the publication of *Tom Brown's Schooldays* in 1857 was simply to accelerate agencies already firmly established in the range of schools.

THE DEVELOPMENT OF ATHLETICISM

The words 'games' and 'athletics' are invariably interchangeable in the nineteenth century. Track and field events, often designated as 'athletic sports', were of little significance in most schools; indeed the annual sports day was chiefly a social occasion, enhanced by the presence of a brass band and lady visitors. In most schools the boys had only a brief period of haphazard and desultory training, though there were some efforts, notably at Uppingham, to raise the status and the seriousness of the occasion. By 'athleticism' is meant the exaltation and disproportionate regard of games, which often resulted in the denigration of academic work and in anti-intellectualism. The extent of the growth of athleticism in the 1860s can be gauged from the reports of the Public School Commissioners and of the Schools Inquiry Commission. The former, reporting in 1864, expressed their firm recognition of the value of games, revealing too their acceptance of the view that the predominant reasons for playing games were the moral and social benefits derived. But already they found cause for regret that in schools where the interest in games was all-absorbing it led to the neglect of schoolwork, they also regretted the introduction of professional coaching in cricket. Nevertheless, they were convinced of the compatibility of distinction in work and in games, and though they regarded the boys' own interest in games as exaggerated, they saw the value of physical activities as an antidote to both over-study and indolence.[25]

Eton, Harrow and Westminster were the schools where disproportionate attention was paid to games. At Eton position and influence in the school were gained almost exclusively by prowess in cricket or rowing. Intellectual achievement was of no significance in the boys' eyes; indeed it was accepted generally, and by the headmaster himself, that success in sport and academic eminence were not compatible because of the severe demands on boys made by coaches in cricket and rowing and by the preparation and concentration needed for academic work. The result was a dichotomy, the King's scholars (who were scholarship-holders and lived in) being distinguished in their studies, and the oppidans (who lived in the town) finding glory in sport. To succeed at games boys spent five hours at practice on each of the three half-days and at least two hours on the whole days; the captain and other keen sportsmen spent five hours each day. Staff attitudes ranged from approval to condemnation of games. Edmund Warre seems to have been the first to express the opinion, commonly held later, that organised games provided the antidote to idleness and 'vice', the Victorian euphemism for homosexual activities; he defended games against criticisms of master-participation and of having adverse effects on academic work. Oscar Browning's plaintive view was that it is 'a most difficult thing at a public school to create a proper appreciation of intellectual distinction', and he lamented that the 'most influential boys in the school are the captains of the boats, and of the eleven, and those who chiefly support them.'[26] Similarly at Harrow proficiency at sport was the criterion of esteem amongst the boys, an illustration being the fact that the athletes had exclusive membership of a select club.

The Commissioners found that balance between play and work which they admired at Winchester and Rugby. At the former, though a keen cricketer might spend an average of three hours a day at the game and though the school was successful at sport, academic work was respected and there was a general interest in scholarship.

Compulsion to play games was not universal at this time. There were no complaints of undue pressure at Eton, where a junior King's scholar stated he was excused football by his senior if he had his schoolwork to do. At Harrow, however, games were compulsory for all boys below the upper fifth unless they had spent three years in the school, though the head boy and the monitors had power to exempt. The juniors were obliged to play and were not simply forced to attend in order to fag for the seniors. The case of W. S. Mayrick at Westminster illustrates both compulsion to play and the severity of punishment invoked by breaking the boys' laws: because he was a member of the eleven he had been compelled to play, and his reluctance had caused attacks to be made upon him, to such an extent that he was removed from the school because of his ill-treatment. The connection between boarding and athleticism is also clearly shown: boys at the day schools did not have the time or opportunity to develop an interest in games detrimental to their academic work. The head-master of Merchant Taylors' suggested that as sons of professional men and merchants, his boys needed a serious attitude to their schoolwork in order to make their way in the world. Some schools, Shrewsbury for example, revealed that they made distinctions between day and boarding boys in games.

The Report of the Public Schools Commissioners also shows the assumption by headmasters of responsibility for providing facilities for physical exercise as part of the increased amenities of the reformed schools. Moberly of Winchester, for example, approved the introduction of separate games of cricket and football for the little boys, and employed a drill-sergeant to remedy postural defects. At Harrow the headmaster paid a rental of £40 a year for the football field, taking over a former responsibility of the boys. He employed a fencing-master and a drill-sergeant, though these activities (and the Corps which existed for military training) were voluntary. Even Kennedy had reorganised games at Shrewsbury so that swimming was taught and a gymnastic apparatus provided. There is evidence that parents simply would not patronise schools which did not reach the standards of accommodation and amenity which they considered necessary. Shrewsbury, Westminster and Charterhouse were severely hampered by cramped quarters; indeed it became clear that the only eventual solution for the low recruitment for most of the city schools was the acquisition of more suitable sites.

The rationalisation of the function of games as a major medium for the achievement of the social and educational aims of the schools was aided by the increasing participation of masters. Masters were already playing in school teams, for the typical 'foreign' matches of this period were against scratch and 'named' teams and were not inter-school games. Masters were also advising and coaching, their participation being generally encouraged by headmasters because of the consequent improvement in school tone and *esprit de corps*. House games were also becoming more organised rather than spontaneous affairs. At Eton for example challenge cups for boating, cricket and football were being played for by 1863. Additional pressures towards compulsory play obviously would be forthcoming as master-involvement and approval grew, especially if the view were to develop that those not wishing to play were 'idlers'.

The exaggerated status already acquired by games at the more aristocratic schools may have had some connection with the attitudes of boys who could depend upon inherited wealth, and who consequently had no need to prepare themselves for a career. At Eton, William (Cory) Johnson believed that the number of oppidans in this category had been greatly exaggerated, and that the greater number of them needed to work for their future success. It seems likely that the greater personal freedom accorded the boys at these schools was of greater importance. The admired balance between work and play at Winchester and Rugby was due to the influence of two strong headmasters, George Moberly and Frederick Temple, who ensured that there was no undue interference from any quarter with the academic work, though the former had to fight continually to restrain the protagonists of sport.

By the time the Report of the Public Schools Commissioners was published in 1864, the monopoly of the schools they investigated, particularly in boarding education, was over. In the same year the Schools Inquiry Commission was established to examine middle-class education, particularly the endowed grammar schools, with whose work there was widespread dissatisfaction. The Commissioners agreed with their immediate predecessors about the advantages of boarding education because of the effect upon the formation of character. As we have seen, examples of the deliberate encouragement of games to improve school discipline had occurred in the 1850s, the most significant being at Marlborough and Uppingham. Edward Thring's example at Uppingham is a most important influence. His evaluation of games was part of his concept of the importance of each individual boy, for he believed all boys should be intelligently cared for whatever their abilities. His ideal was a balance: '. . . it is a noble thing to endure and to train the body, as it is to work hard and train the mind'.[27] And he saw

> . . . many a boy whom we must put at a low level in school redeems his self-respect by the praise bestowed upon him as a game player, and the balance of manliness and intellect is more impartially kept.[28]

He set great store upon a high standard of provision, aiming at 'as perfect an equipment as possible in cricket and football grounds and fives courts'. In 1859 he opened the first 'covered' gymnasium in an English public school, appointing a German, G. H. C. Beisiegel, to teach gymnastics. He invented his own game of football for the school, based mainly on the Eton field game, with some of the modifications of the Rugby game. He set a stirring example in the toughest activities, noting in 1862:

> . . . was asked to play football today; the Sixth against the school. Did so, though I have long ago given up regular playing; it is too severe. Had a first-rate game. They play a great deal better than when I left off, indeed they play beautifully. I could not help think-ing with some pride what headmaster of a great school had even played a match of football before. Would either dignity or shin suffer it? I think not.[29]

In his evidence to the commission Thring referred to the 'thoroughly friendly' relationships between masters and boys, stressing the value of the participation of the former in games. Games, too, were given the credit for the good relations between boarders and day-boys. Thring's influence grew steadily, for he was consulted about such schemes as the foundation of Clifton and Fettes, while his fame grew markedly after his establishment of the Headmasters' Conference in 1869 and after his successful transference of his school to Borth in 1876. By that date, however, he was concerned to restrict the importance of games in his school.

The schools examined by the Commissioners included those where the 'current muscular theories' were well established and others which for a variety of reasons made no provision at all for the boys to exercise or play games. The association of playground provision with boarding accommodation is seen in a large number of instances. Often the restricted use of these facilities underlies the division between boarders and day boys. The latter were often foundationers, either paying low fees or no fees under the provision of the deeds of endowment of the school, while the boarders' fees were regarded as a necessary supplement to the headmaster's stipend. It was common for the headmaster himself to pay for the provision of a playground and to hire a playing field for the exclusive use of his boarders. Indeed the selective criteria placed highest by parents were exclusiveness, household arrangements and sporting amenities.

The general picture of developments in the 1860s is of games firmly established, financed by the boys' subscriptions, the interest of heads and assistant masters being reflected in their financial support, their playing for school cricket teams and their participation in the organisation and administration of sport by serving on games committees. Before the end of the decade, 'foreign' games were being played in cricket, while efforts were being made to adopt common acceptable codes of laws in football so that regular fixtures against clubs and schools could be established. Gymnastic apparatus had been introduced in many schools with ex-NCOs in charge, or alternatively senior boys took charge both of the apparatus and of the coaching of their juniors. Swimming baths were being provided, though swimming commonly took place at the nearest river or suitable pond. Rowing, too, had become an organised activity at schools appropriately sited.

In the 1870s the interest in games was intensified. A clear, chronological account of the changes involved is not possible because of the haphazard and individual nature of the development. The excesses of athleticism are perhaps seen at their worst in H. A. Vachell's novel of Harrow life, *The Hill*. Eton, under Edmund Warre, is however held generally to be the apogee of the athletically dominated school. Warre's influence was strongest during the headship of Hornby (1868–84). He succeeded to the headship, but not before he had been attacked vituperatively in *The Times*:

> ... for the last quarter of a century he has made no mark as a scholar, a preacher or a man of letters. His name is associated with no question of educational reform; on the other hand he is well known as the best rowing coach in England and as an able field-officer of Volunteers. He is an oppidan of oppidans.[30]

This and similar attacks were not in fact directed against his athleticism and his militarism, but were the protests of those who wished to retain the dominance of Collegers and Kingsmen at Eton. Warre's work at Eton illustrates the stricter control of boys' lives which became a widespread feature at this time. He was concerned to organise the leisure time of the boys so that none would escape compulsory games: his view of games as an antidote to undesirable activities has already been noted, and now by the employment of rigorous organisation he wished to remove opportunities for 'vice'. But his outlook was narrow, so that he distrusted those who did not conform to his stereotype. Similarly at Rugby, John Percival, headmaster from 1887 to 1895, initiated reforms to develop a highly regimented school life. Boys were to be given so detailed a timetable that there would be no opportunity for getting into evil ways.[31] J. H. Simpson describes the over-regulation and excessive games of the period, seeing the real reason to be fear of wrong-doing and specifically *suspicio sexualis*.[32] A change of emphasis characteristic of many schools occurs at Winchester, where George Ridding's organisation and creation of new facilities established the importance of games. The concentrated attention given to sport is reflected in the success of the school at cricket from 1888–92 and the continuation of that success until 1914.[33] Evidence of the primacy of achievement in sport during this period has also been deduced from the choice as prefects of those whose assets seemed limited to physical prowess.[34] This transfer of prefectorial power from the scholars to the sportsmen is indeed a common feature of the time.[35]

Where the old-established public schools led, many younger

establishments followed eagerly. The Commissioners appointed under the Endowed Schools Act of 1869 effected many hundreds of schemes of reform, which resulted in the improvement of many grammar schools, some being able to climb into the ranks of the public schools. The whole structure was intended to benefit the middle classes and to reinforce existing class distinctions. Foundations such as Marlborough, Wellington and Clifton had been able to build their own traditions and school spirit within a very few years. At Clifton, football was compulsory by 1868, and cricket became so pre-eminent that even the introduction of a cadet corps and the provision of a new gymnasium in 1874 were regarded by some as a threat to its position. Sir Francis Newbolt wrote of his schooldays there: 'The real summit of ambition was to be in the Eleven. . . . The real interest in life was still cricket.'[36] Thring's fears that cricket might be made a god were amply justified.

The amount of athleticism appears to have been greatest in schools which were successful in reaching the top ranks. The development of games in schools other than the most exclusive rarely remained for long entirely in the boys' hands, masters and boys often exercising joint control in games committees, and the overriding authority of the headmaster being frequently asserted. Invariably games developed later in day schools and without the intensity of interest found in the boarding schools. Many of the day grammar schools (eg those at Hull and Bristol) had to fight hard to survive, relying upon Kensington Science grants and, after 1902, upon local-authority aid.

Though the number of schools of the grammar type had expanded greatly from 1868 to the end of the century, they still catered for only a very small proportion of the population, and their position was threatened by the new 'higher grade' secondary schools created by the School Boards. The Education Act of 1902, in securing the abolition of the latter, accentuated the difference between elementary and secondary education. The new secondary schools conformed closely to the pattern established by the traditional grammar schools. Certainly in physical education there was a remarkable broadening of facilities, team games quickly becoming an integral part of life. Such developments are exemplified in Norwich, where the City of Norwich School, opened in 1910, was an amalgam of the Higher Grade School and a 'commercial' school. The only facility in the former had been a small playground where each boy had ten minutes' drill a day, whereas the new school had a gymnasium and playing fields, so that a full programme of physical education could be initiated straightaway. Again, typically, the pattern of internally organised games based upon 'house' divisions was introduced.

The pattern of life and the established values of the public schools had a marked influence upon the girls' boarding schools established in the seventies and eighties. St Leonard's School, founded at St Andrews in 1877, created the precedent, adopting many of the features of the boys' schools: an hour and a half a day was allocated to games, which included cricket, golf, tennis, hockey and fives.

Games were accorded an equal importance at Wycombe Abbey, established in the south as a replica of St Leonard's,[37] and even more at Roedean School, Brighton, opened in 1885; the first prospectus stated 'Special pains will be taken to guard against overwork, and from two to three hours daily will be allotted to outdoor exercise and games'. Inspired by the Reverend Edmund Luce, a double-Blue, cricket became a seriously regarded occupation.[38] Miss Lawrence, the headmistress, describes how the machinery of the boys' schools was taken to Roedean, with similar pressures for conformity. The games committee organised play, awarded colours and enforced compulsory attendance. For those excused games on medical grounds the alternative was a walk, but the choice must have had attendant unpleasantness, for 'many who dislike the games, dislike the walk more and choose the lesser evil'. Miss Lawrence valued games not only as the finest form of exercise but also for their pre-eminence in the training of character. Indeed she was quite immoderate in her evaluation of their influence on the development of the national character, setting an especially high store on the moral value of cricket.[39]

Many others followed, for by 1898 there were over eighty endowed secondary schools for girls, and in Miss Lawrence's view very few of them had not established games as an important part of school life. The boarding schools followed the lead of the boys' schools in stressing games facilities in their prospectuses, though it is obvious that the new pattern was at least an improvement on the old routine of stuffy rooms and crocodile walks. Games rarely attained the status of isolated splendour that they achieved in boys' schools; at Roedean, for example, they were part of a full programme of physical activity. The whole school had an hour's gymnastics a week and almost all the girls could swim, proficiency awards and colours stimulating a high standard. The early establishment of the women's physical training colleges—the first had been set up by Miss Bergman in 1885 and by 1905 there were six specialist colleges—brought a steady supply of fully trained women to teach physical education, and the paucity of suitable occupations for women meant that many of real ability were recruited to middle-class schools.

Though there were critics both within and outside the schools who condemned the constriction which resulted from the stress upon games and the demanded conformity, it was not until after World War I that a more tolerant attitude prevailed. Indeed the intense patriotism of the pre-war period resulted not only in more military training and the foundation of the Officers' Training Corps, but also a renewed emphasis upon games. In 1917 Colonel Jerrard, a survivor of the Ashanti Expedition, in exhorting the boys of Norwich School to row harder, expressed his view that 'the soldier boy who is no good at sports is less than useless as a leader of men'. Such sentiments reflect the sense of mission and self-confidence of the public schools during these years.

After World War I, in the spate of criticism of pre-war institutions, the public schools were prominent targets. There was to be no return to the 'security, stability and certainty' of the pre-war era. Progressive forces were at work within the schools engendering greater informality in relationships between masters and boys and greater kindliness amongst the boys themselves. The interests of the older boys were broadened to include public and political affairs, while there grew an increasing awareness of the needs of other sections of society. Many wished to see a more liberal view of sport adopted, with the traditional team games becoming less important and a wider variety of physical pastime encouraged. Old attitudes, however, died hard. After World War II the general uncertainty of the place of public schools was the reason for growing demands for freedom within the schools, and for less respect for certain institutions and traditions. A more mature outlook resulted in a more rational appreciation of the relative value of achievement in sport. At their best games became regarded as part of that 'sound environment for growth' schools should provide. As alternatives to a wide range of games, outdoor pursuits, social service and voluntary service were developed.

It is difficult to achieve a balanced estimate of the effect of the exalted status of games upon individuals. When written in retrospect, the portrayal of a boy's views of life is often idealised and dominated by nostalgia, or else merely condemnatory. Hornung's portrait of life at Uppingham is reasonably accurate as a record of the mores of junior boys in the late nineteenth-century public school, showing especially their reverence for athletic heroes, but when his subjects become senior members of the community the author's sense of reality fails him and he exaggerates incidents for the sake of dramatic effect.[40] The impact of the values of an English public school upon an alien spirit is revealed in the account of Alfred Mond's schooldays at Cheltenham (1878–80). Used to rigorous intellectual discipline he committed the *faux pas* of writing his first essay in blank verse, and he was no good at games:

> Old Cheltonians recall a pathetic figure of the boy kicking a football, alone, hour after hour, so that he might become competent, so that he might take his place with the English boys. It was part of his struggle towards the English idea.[41]

The full diaries kept by W. R. Grove for his last three years at Uppingham (they are also the last years of Thring's long regime), illustrate one boy's reactions to aspects of school life in a most revealing way. The son of a Huntingdonshire doctor, he was destined to follow his father's career and he realised fully that his primary purpose at school was to acquire the necessary academic knowledge. He was no great athlete and seemed somewhat handicapped by a slight physique and rather weak eyesight. He was clearly keen to be as prominent a player in school cricket and football as he possibly could be. The summit of his achievement was to be captain of the IVth eleven; nor were his ambitions in football realised: 'In afternoon there was a match 5 form v School, I was not playing for either side; so now I suppose I finished my career as a footballist: my dream of the 15 is as smoke.' As first school began at 7.30 am in winter and 7 am in summer, there was plenty of time for games on each weekday. Boys were invariably free from midday until late afternoon, while there were a fair number of days which were in effect full holidays. Grove took a keen interest in the fortunes of the school team when inter-school matches were played, illustrating the importance of these occasions for the boys and revealing the enthusiasm which greeted success and its accompanying enhancement of prestige. He took part in the full range of physical activities, playing fives, tennis, swimming, running in paper-chases and in heats for the sports, as well as playing team games. He gives no impression of compulsion to play, indeed he seems to decide for himself whether to do so or not, particularly when in the sixth form. He had the English schoolboy's traditional apathy towards gymnastics, finding a wide variety of reasons to justify his absence from the sessions held at 8 o'clock in the evening. His other interests included music, drama and the assistant editorship of the magazine. He read avidly from time to time, completing twenty-nine works by popular authors in 1886. His own view of his schoolwork is shown in his description of his leaving interview with Thring,

He said he intended to give me the Praeposter's Leaving Medal, but it was with misgivings, as I had only done sufficient work here to satisfy an easy conscience: this is because I had not attended properly to his talks on divinity: tho' he talked all through nominally of all my work, yet I knew he really meant divinity, and to that I own to only having done sufficient work etc. But in everything else I think all round I have tried my best: of course sometimes I have scamped work, but usually I have done my best.[42]

DEVELOPMENTS IN PHYSICAL EDUCATION OVERSEAS

It is interesting to compare developments in England with those in continental countries and in the United States. Matthew Arnold made special reports of continental systems of physical education for the consideration of the Endowed Schools' Commissioners. He found much to be commended in the gymnastics he had seen, though he had strong reservations about their acceptability in English public schools. Of French boys he wrote that they

... seem to enjoy themselves with great spirit, and their gymnastics are probably a better physical training for the short time they have to give to exercise than our boys' amusements would be; but they do not, in general, to my thinking look so fresh, happy and healthy as our public school boys.

His reservations were:

... and the spirit and gaiety of an English boy do not go with him into his exercise, he flags in it, if he does not feel he is at play and free in it; thus it has been observed that gymnastics do not flourish in our schools, they are too much of a drill or a lesson.[43]

He observed too that all the boys learnt gymnastics and singing at the Prussian gymnasien, and found that the impulse and ideals of the Philanthropinum at Dessau were bearing fruit in the Realschulen. Of gymnastics he wrote:

The Germans, as is well known, now cultivate gymnastics in their schools with great care. Since 1842 gymnastics have been made a regular part of a Central Turenstalt at Berlin, with 18 civilian pupils who are being trained expressly to supply model teachers of gymnastics for the public schools . . .

Nothing, however, will make an ex-schoolboy of one of the great English schools regard the gymnastics of a foreign school without a slight feeling of wonder and compassion, so much more animating and interesting do the games of his remembrance seem to him. This much, however, I will say; if boys have long work hours, or if they work hard, gymnastics probably do more for their physical health in the comparatively short time allocated to recreation than anything else could. . . . For little boys, again, I am inclined to think that the carefully taught gymnastics of a foreign school are better than the lounging shivering about, which used often at our great schools to be the portion of those who had not yet come to full age for games.[44]

Thring's example of appointing a German teacher of gymnastics at Uppingham in 1859 was not emulated, the usual pattern in schools being the employment of drill-sergeants for the corps and also for physical exercises, boxing, fencing and single-stick. Even at Uppingham, gymnastics had very minor status in comparison with games, and it seems that in most schools the gymnastics taught by the drill-sergeants were regarded as unimportant. The increase of interest in gymnastic exercises, with the consequent increase of the time allocated, was a marked feature of many schools during the years between the two world wars. In the United States during the Civil War the stress upon drill is seen to have prevented the acceptance of physical education in the land-grant colleges, but by the end of the century less than 5 per cent of the high schools gave military instruction.[45] This period saw a tremendous growth of games and sport in American society, reflected in a comparable growth of interest within schools and colleges. Again it seems clear that the original impetus for games and sport came from the students, rather than from the college and school authorities, and that there were problems associated with over-emphasis and professionalism. Professionalism is clearly the dominant feature in the growth of intercollegiate football teams to business concerns of such dimensions that their annual budgets approached a million dollars, while such support and interest was generated in the 1920s and 1930s that the sport was called 'a national religion'.[46]

How then may the influence and effect of the development of games in the English boarding schools—both the public schools and the schools which copied them—be judged? There was undoubtedly an over-emphasis accompanied by a narrowness of outlook, an intolerance of alternatives and an unwholesome concentration upon the achieving of success. The 'worst feature' of the education that resulted was 'that in its efforts to achieve manliness by stressing the importance of playing games, it fell into the (opposite) error of failing to make boys into men at all'.[47]

As more tolerant attitudes and broader outlooks overcame the strong conservatism of the schools, a less emotive and more rational appreciation of the value of physical activities was achieved in the most resistant quarters. To innumerable boys and girls, games brought healthy exercise and pleasure, while schools benefited in discipline, in community of interest and in better relationships between teachers and taught.

So the development of organised sport may also be seen as the particular contribution of Victorian England, the value of which is difficult to estimate:

The physical benefit to populations becoming everywhere more urbanised must be great. The psychological advantage in a world where initiative and individuality are tending to be ironed out by mechanisation and mass production will not I believe be less.[48]

2

Athleticism: the ethical and sociological background

It is this character-building which is the great feature and the glory of English public schools.

> Dr Inskip in his final report of 1913,
> quoted in J. Booth, *Framlingham College—The First Sixty Years*

Many influences, both within the schools and outside, caused games to achieve that exaggerated status associated with the term 'athleticism'. With the reform of the traditional public schools and the establishment of numerous new foundations, a number of secular influences helped to change established values, a change epitomised by David Newsome (*Godliness and Good Learning*, 1961) as the transmutation from 'Godliness and Good Learning' to 'Godliness and Manliness'. Official acceptance of games and master-participation were soon followed by a rationalisation of their function, for they were seen to make a major contribution to the development of 'character', for a long time the major purpose of public-school education. Games were linked with character not only because they were seen to engender the qualities of courage, co-operation and initiative and to discourage laziness, but also because they were viewed as an aspect of a boy's service to his community—to his house and school. Boys themselves thought that the playing of games in this spirit ought to be encouraged as a preferred alternative to compulsory participation. The first issue of the magazine of The Leys School at Cambridge warned boys that a spirit of service should be evident in their playing of games, 'the victory . . . belongs to no single member of the eleven. Let there be no strife for personal glorification.' Archbishop Temple, speaking at Uppingham in 1936, also attributed the stress upon games to this reason:

> . . . he did see the value of games because participation in them was a kind of service [of the boy's] to his community, his school; while the contribution of the scholar was not so evident. That was the ground of the greater interest that there undoubtedly was in athletic than in scholastic successes.

MUSCULAR CHRISTIANITY

Thomas Arnold inspired boys with ideals of service, but as already seen, he would never have countenanced the suggestion that intellectual achievement should be subordinated to physical prowess.[1] That such a change in values occurred is in part due to the work and influence of the Muscular Christians. Charles Kingsley is held to be the first of these to state views which were later to gain wide acceptance. As a student at Cambridge, Kingsley participated vigorously in many kinds of sport. In his writing he exalted physical prowess and national pride, seeing 'manliness' as the antidote to the effeminacy of the Tractarians, whose advocacy of celibacy he abhorred. Another aspect of his 'manliness' was a fervid patriotism. Kingsley was also influenced by the Christian Socialism of F. D. Maurice, joining in 1847 a group of young men gathered by Maurice at Lincoln's Inn to do social and religious work among the poor in neighbouring parishes.

Kingsley's personal preference seemed to be for spontaneous vigorous activities in a natural environment, rather than in organised games. He was concerned to give his own children a happy childhood and to inspire in them a love of nature. But he also expressed his strong convictions of the functions of health education and games in schools. The former he advocated as a remedy for the corruption by sedentary living of the physical inheritance of 'our hardy forefathers . . . one of the mightiest and most capable races which the world has ever seen'. He rejected notions that games were not beneficial:

> . . . boys and masters alike know that games, do not in the long run, interfere with a boy's work; that the same boy will often excel in both, that the games keep him in health for his work; that the spirit with which he takes to his games when in the lower school, is a fair test of the spirit which he will take to his work when he rises into the higher school; and that nothing is worse for a boy than to fall into the loafing, tuckshop-haunting set, who neither play hard nor work hard, and are usually extravagant, and often vicious. Moreover, they know well that games conduce not merely to physical, but to moral health; that in the playing field boys acquire virtues which no book can give them; not merely daring and endurance, but, better still, temper, self-restraint, fairness, honour, unenvious approbation of another's success, and all that 'give and take' of life which stand a man in good stead when he goes forth into the world, and without which, indeed, his success is always maimed and partial.[2]

The specific exaltation of games, however, was the contribution of Thomas Hughes in *Tom Brown's Schooldays*, the success and significance of which has been examined. Hughes praises the virtues of the manly pastimes of English village life, especially wrestling and back-swording, stating that if these were to be replaced it must be by activities equally strenuous and demanding physically. To Hughes men were fundamentally equal, the true basis of comparison being physical courage, endurance and other aspects of 'character'. Consequently he viewed the main purpose of education as being not to provide 'the good scholar', but 'a brave, helpful, truth-telling Englishman, and a gentleman and a Christian'. In his own schooldays at Rugby the twin formative influences producing the desired result were those of Arnold himself and of organised games. At Rugby, Hughes had been captain of Bigside, the senior game of football, and of the eleven. At Oxford, he had played in the university eleven and stroked the boat-race crew. From his own experience he was convinced of the moral as well as the physical value of games. Victory was

won even against great odds by virtue of courage and steadfast-
ness; thus the School-house, under the leadership of the headmaster, won at football because of the greater community feeling
amongst its boys. Similarly cricket is exalted by being viewed as
an 'institution' rather than as a game, its value being the discipline
and team spirit engendered. To Hughes these were the qualities
necessary in an English gentleman, for the additional value of
games was their inculcation of patriotic feeling; concern for house
and school was linked with national pride.

Clearly there were marked distinctions between Arnold's view
of games and that of Hughes. Arnold's belief that secular interests
and even physical activity have spiritual value can be seen to lead
to Kingsley's preaching of 'the divineness of the whole manhood',
but the change of emphasis between Arnold's beliefs and the
standpoint of Hughes results in a completely different conception.
Arnold's stress upon academic achievement is lost completely, to
be replaced by an anti-intellectualism. The portrayal of Arnold by
Hughes was accepted, because of the popularity and appeal of his
novel and because of the power of his writing. For, although as a
schoolboy Hughes had not been close to Arnold as A. P. Stanley
had, it is Hughes who communicates more effectively Arnold's
powerful influence over boys in his picture of

> ... him who stood there Sunday after Sunday witnessing and plead-
> ing for his Lord, the King of righteousness and love and glory,
> with whose spirit he was filled, and in whose power he spoke ...
> The true sort of Captain too for a boys' army ... it was his
> thoroughness and undaunted courage which more than anything
> else won his way to the hearts of the great mass of those on whom
> he left his mark, and made them believe first in him, and then in
> his Master.[3]

This simplified picture of Arnold has been seen by Asa Briggs
as having contributed to the development of the public school as
a national institution.[4] The social mission of the reformed schools
and the newly established schools had two aspects, the creation of
'gentlemen' and the mixing of the sons of the old upper classes

with the sons of the new middle classes. Hughes's contribution was to make the schools popular with the middle classes. His ideas were disseminated widely through the popularity of *Tom Brown's Schooldays* and became a model for the public schools expanding to meet the demands of the new middle classes enjoying the mid-Victorian prosperity. Hughes's compound of manly self-reliance and patriotism linked with Christianity was more easily understood and far more acceptable than Arnold's radicalism, piety and intellectualism. Hughes also contributed to the work of the Working Men's College founded in 1854, setting an example of service to less privileged sections of the community. Here he taught boxing and exercises on the parallel bars, later organising cricket and rowing clubs, out of which grew the college Corps of Volunteers of which he was commandant. Of Hughes's later writings, *Tom Brown at Oxford* is the most important. In this work sport is advocated as an antidote for the malaise afflicting undergraduate life and again its moral purpose is stressed.

While Hughes was writing of undergraduate life, Leslie Stephen was creating a new conception of the Cambridge don. Though in his early years he had been delicate he took up rowing when an undergraduate, achieving great success later as a coach. Stephen was a remarkable don because of the personal interest he took in the undergraduates. He lived with the students of Trinity Hall as one of them; he founded the Cambridge University sports, winning the mile and two-mile races himself, supported the Oxford *v* Cambridge sports in 1864 and was one of the initiators of the Volunteer Movement (mentioned below). He was a formidable walker, inspiring students to follow his example. Stephen saw that many exaggerated and unfounded claims were being made for athletics, but he preferred the English student to his continental counterpart, finding compensation for intellectual shortcomings in the development of 'character': 'We don't turn out many very learned men—the temptations to practical life in England are too overpowering, but we turn out plenty of hard-headed energetic men, fit to fight a good battle in the world.'[5]

Stephen championed the cause of the undergraduates, wishing to reform a system which he saw condemned them to frustration and boredom, which in turn were the cause of immature behaviour. His attempted reforms failed, his proposed changes being attacked by Dr Mayor of St John's as being inspired by a 'pestilent muscular Christianity'. Yet his is a seminal influence leading to reform:

> The active participation of college fellows in sports . . . is part of the same change of attitude which led those thinkers to stress the importance of teaching . . . Dons began to respond to the external pressures on the university, to demands that Cambridge broaden its curriculum, remove its civil disabilities and lower its expenses in order to attract more students.[6]

Kingsley, Hughes and Stephen were not the first to exalt the 'manly virtues', and it is difficult to estimate the extent of their influence, yet there is evidently a clear link between the ideals predetermined by them and the later developments in the public schools. As Newsome states, 'Thirty or forty years later, the same ideals or something very like them might be taken to be the creed of the typical housemaster of the typical public school.'[7] The ideals expressed by the three were popular with those who saw that England's future lay in the expansion of her influence overseas, for the qualities of physical courage and fortitude, linked with self-reliance and fervent patriotism were just the qualities needed by potential Empire builders. It was not a simple one-way influence, as has been pointed out:

> In the making of the balance [of Victorian society] and the formation of character necessary to sustain it, the public school was a key institution, and changes in the public schools were responsible in some measure at least for the adaptations of old institutions to meet new needs. The idea of the school influenced the idea of the nation, sometimes very directly.[8]

The Muscular Christians may be held to be partly responsible for the subsequent development of athleticism, and even Hughes regretted the later extremes. Yet undoubted benefits also followed from their work and example. Canon Raven has paid handsome tribute to Hughes's great personal contribution to the achievements of the Christian Socialists. He worked with steadfast enthusiasm, setting an ideal of service to the working class and bringing a zest for life and spiritual values. Physical activities, initiated by the influences of Kingsley and Hughes and those who followed them were often the first, and most valued, link between those with privileged backgrounds who chose to work in poor neighbourhoods and those whose lot in life they sought to improve. Muscular Christianity can also be seen as providing a necessary counterblast to the cloistered, self-conscious ascetic religiosity of the Tractarians.

THE MILITARY INFLUENCE

Just as the later exaltation of games was presaged by the high moral value placed upon them by the Muscular Christians, so their status was enhanced by the high regard accorded them in the development of patriotic militarism. By the middle years of the century a change in mood was evident, attention was focused overseas and the nation acquired 'an aggressive imperial self-consciousness' which reached its peak in 1859. Distrust of France, occasioned by Napoleon III's Italian policy, caused a great upsurge of anti-French sentiment and a determination to build up a position of strength. This resulted in the strengthening of the navy and coastal fortifications, with the official sponsorship of the Volunteer Rifle Club Movement in May 1859. Enthusiastic support was gained, 60,000 men enrolling within a year.[9] In the following year Lord Elcho initiated the movement for the introduction of military drill to the public schools. The response was ready, corps being established quickly at Eton, Winchester, Harrow, Rugby and Shrewsbury. Units were also formed at many of the newer foundations and at proprietary schools. However, after the first surge of enthusiasm had waned, the Volunteer Movement did not make a marked impact on the schools until the revival of interest which came with the Boer War at the turn of the century. The chief attraction to boys was the target shooting, for they found the drill irksome. To spur recruitment Charles Evans reorganised the Eton Corps in 1863, but in 1867 Edmund Warre had to repeat the exercise, linking the corps with the Shooting XI and leasing a rifle range at Chalvey. The problem of recruitment remained, though Warre was able to inject interest periodically. Annual camps, begun in 1872, were popular, as were joint activities with other units.[10] The corps grew in strength at the 'top' schools from the 1880s until their reorganisation in 1908.

Warre saw the corps as another means of occupying idle boys, giving those who were not sportsmen something to do. He valued drill as a 'gymnastic exercise', but considered it could be 'fatal' to make it compulsory. Though the corps does not seem to have been made officially compulsory in any school, in the later period pressures were such that in many places not to join was unthinkable. Competitive interest was engendered by the Ashburton shoots, but few schools, other than the major foundations, had units which prospered throughout these years. As might be expected there was greater support at schools with a military orientation; thus at Cheltenham the unit formed in 1862 was later changed into an Engineer Corps for the benefit of boys preparing for Woolwich. With the advent of the corps there came also the employment of ex-service physical-training instructors who, as already noted, taught, coached and organised 'minor' sports such as boxing, swimming, fencing, single-stick and gymnastics (indoor gymnasiums being found commonly after 1870). But neither these nor corps activities could rival the status of the major games. At Clifton the introduction of the corps (as of the gymnasium) was resisted by those who saw in its activities a challenge to the concentration on cricket. Indeed the chief means of giving the impress of patriotism and teaching the qualities of leadership which would be required in a future war were seen to be games, not the corps, Sir Henry Newbolt's poem 'Vitaï Lampada' being the ultimate expression of this belief.

The emphasis upon sport in the schools and upon imperial

service was reinforced by the development of sport generally and by the growth of imperialism. The spread of team games throughout the community dates from the 1870s. The Saturday half-day was gained for the working man, and this was the spur to the rapid spread of games to the working class. There was a rapid growth of clubs and leagues, religious organisations having an important role in these early developments. With the leagues came spectator support and professionalism, the nationally organised Football League being founded in 1888. Interest in sport was stimulated by the spread of popular sporting publications, while public interest reinforced the enthusiasm of boys at school. The last two decades of the century saw also the extensive growth of the Empire and a growing support for imperialism. Both political parties were wooing the working-class electorate with programmes combining the appeal of imperialism with social reform. The enfranchisement of the working class in 1867 had been followed by the growth of socialism, internationalist in outlook, which B. Semmel sees as causing widespread suspicion among the upper and middle classes that the increasingly socialist working class would be unreliable in a future war. Hence they must be won over by a programme of social reform so that they would see that they had most to gain from a policy based upon national and imperial interests.[11] Imperialism was sponsored at a variety of levels, at the worst a crude unrealistic jingoism, which ignored constantly Kipling's emphasis on 'the moral responsibility, on duty and service, on the obligations of Empire'.[12]

Imperialism in society heightened during the South African War with resulting effects in the schools. In 1900, after the first disasters had caused consternation at home, Warre addressed the Royal United Services Institution, indicating the high proportion of casualties among officers and the shortage of officers in the Militia and Volunteers. He described the support he had gained from the Headmasters' Conference for the extension of military training in schools and he now asked the government for an Act to put into effect the training envisaged. From 1902 to 1914 Lord

Roberts and the National Service League were calling for the introduction of conscription, and allied with this campaign was the encouragement of rifle clubs, reflected at Uppingham School in the requirement that every boy should pass a shooting test. The schools responded promptly from 1900, defunct corps being revived and new units established. A good example is found at Gresham's School, being revived as a public school during this period. Here the corps was given a very important place in school life, so that a visiting speaker in 1909 could express the hope that 'Lord Roberts will some day come here and find what an immense deal has been done to develop in the best possible way the martial spirit of this School'.[13]

The schools did not receive the support that Warre asked for in 1900, but had to wait for Haldane's reforms of 1907. This created the territorial force, as part of which Officers Training Corps were set up in the public school and universities. In 1917 the War Office gave increased recognition to the work done in schools by allowing boys recommended as likely to make efficient officers to stay at school until they were eighteen and a half, provided they did ten hours' military training per week.

Increased support for the activities of the corps did not diminish the importance of games; indeed the regard for the benefits to be gained from them seems to have been enhanced. This was expressed clearly in an article in a school magazine in 1914:

> There can be no doubt that our Public school games and physical training are, to a large extent, responsible for the making of good fighting men. That they should cease to exist would be a calamity which even the most ardent militarist would deplore ... We ought, therefore, to consider football, hockey, cricket etc., as part of the preparation which all British patriots are called upon to make at the present time.[14]

Despite Kipling's preference for the barbarian pursuits of hunting and poaching as more appropriate and realistic forms of training, the major team games had become firmly linked with the development of qualities necessary for military service.

Pressures within the schools themselves also influenced the development of athleticism. In England it was primarily a phenomenon associated with boarding education. Pressures are obviously greater in a closed society, values are heightened, a rarified atmosphere is more easily created and there is consequently a greater likelihood of excess.[15] Boarding life accentuated the pressures to conform to the ideal, which was conceptualised in terms of the 'gentleman' and in the development of 'character'.[16] The public schools élitist education placed a premium upon status, while their role in producing public servants resulted in stress upon service to the community and team spirit. The totality of the education of the boarding school accentuated the stress. In the late nineteenth and early twentieth centuries headmasters frequently had to tread a difficult path between sponsoring the social values offered by their schools on the one hand and avoiding the excesses associated with the cult of games on the other. As the headmaster's prestige and income was based upon the success of his school, he too was under pressure to conform to established values. Just as the values of the schools changed, so, it has been noted, did the criteria for the selection and appointment of headmasters:

> . . . the prestige of a headmaster came to be based less upon his scholarship . . . but upon his organisational powers; his capacity for maintaining and developing the 'tone' of his school and for fostering its corporate life through athletics and out-of-school activities.[17]

Examples of participation in the playing and organisation of games were set by famous headmasters. Where the headmaster led, other masters were constrained to follow, for until the passing of the Endowed Schools (Masters) Act of 1908 they had merely the standing of his employed servants. The joint control of masters and boys of the organisation of games was often exercised in Games Committees, and it is clear that the overriding authority of the headmaster was frequently asserted. The archetypal figure of the headmaster in the latter half of the nineteenth century was the venerated doctor of divinity, still able to 'turn an arm' in the nets on the eve of retirement. His replacement was frequently a man with a distinguished record in games at the university.

The establishment and growth of authority of housemasters had also resulted from the reform of the schools during the middle years of the nineteenth century. Increasing size of schools meant the delegation of authority from headmasters to housemasters, for the house was evidently a more efficient disciplinary unit. There was not the modern restriction of tenure of office so that in many schools the power and prestige of housemasters grew to such proportions that they achieved a dominant position. For most boys games meant house games and house matches. Their main interest in school matches often centred around the performance of members of particular houses in the school teams. Games were exalted because superiority at them provided tangible evidence of the superiority of the house. Housemasters had the authority to wield immense influence—and there were many to follow Edward Bowen's high evaluation of the place of games in house life at Harrow School.

The major role accorded to boy authority in the schools is evidently most important. There was a tradition of boy independence, especially in the 'top' schools while the initial development of games was the result of the boys' own endeavours. At Rugby, for example, the rules of Rugby Football were the concern of the boys, so that when a masters' meeting decided to discontinue the match against the sixth form in 1900 it was criticised strongly as an intervention in boys' rights. As games became more sophisticated the assistance of masters for coaching became necessary, but the ultimate responsibility was claimed to be the boys'. In 1937 the senior boys declared that the assistance of masters in out-of-school activities 'should be given only when invited and should be in a purely advisory capacity'.[18] Much of this independence of outlook has persisted in the more exclusive schools until the present day. In other schools, however, the usual control of games is exercised by a joint staff-pupil games committee, the head-master having the last word.

There are also ubiquitous references in the literature to the changes in the nature of boy authority, seen in the older schools in the transfer of prefectorial authority from the scholars of the sixth form to the games players, and in the preferential treatment of sportsmen in the newer schools. Thus was initiated the 'Rule of the Bloods', whose superior status was emphasised by elaborate ritual and by paraphernalia of dress. In the rigidly structured society of the schools, the top places were accorded to the athletes, and the conservative outlook of the authorities and of the boys en masse enshrined the practices with which such status was asso-ciated as traditions to be handed on. At house level the organisa-tion of games and practices was invariably in the hands of the boys, who enforced conformity and applied sanctions, and against whose authority there was no appeal.

The participation of masters in games and coaching resulted in the appointment of men primarily for the contribution they could make to sport—the games masters. The life of Tom Collins illus-trates such a career. He entered Cambridge in 1859, spending his time rowing and playing cricket and billiards. His academic achievement was to reach the middle of the second class by virtue of 'last-minute cram'. He had no prospects of a career but was appointed to King Edward's School, Birmingham, on the strength of his cricket Blue. After eight years there he served as headmaster of the grammar school at Newport in Shropshire for thirty-three years.[19] By the 1880s and 90s a marked change in the type of assistant master being appointed is noticeable: graduates from Oxford and Cambridge were prominent sportsmen, while a common feature is the appointment to staffs of old boys who have been outstanding sportsmen at school and then at university. The cycle of schoolboy sportsman, university sportsman and school-master sportsman was created.

The growth of sport at the universities also reinforced the mystique attached to games at schools. Letters from the schools' correspondents at the universities invariably seem to be almost exclusively preoccupied with sport, either with the progress and achievements of university teams, or with the sporting activities of those old boys currently in residence. The great value of games at the university was urged upon the boys of Uppingham, who were warned that a successful academic career at school did not guarantee success at the university, but were told to emulate the ideal of Muscular Christianity:

> Who then are the men who succeed at the 'varsity? and elsewhere? Those who remember they have a body, mind and a soul, men who are good all round. The Football blue rises tenfold in the general estimation, when it is reported that his coach expects him to come out in the top half of the Wranglers; and the scholar has an immense pull over his spectacled and knock-kneed rival, when he gets a seat in his College boat . . . it is remarkable how few do really well in the Schools or Triposes who do not to some extent shine in games as well.[20]

The old boys exerted another strong influence reinforcing established values and resisting change. This decisive effect is seen at Uppingham in 1870: Thring had allowed the appointment of a cricket professional for alternate years only, but he gave way to the boys' requests for an appointment each year when influential old boys added their support. Two years later the headmaster was persuaded to appoint an additional residential coach, and an old boy who was the school's most eminent cricketer chose and paid for the professional, winning Thring's reluctant consent. Many old boys gave generously to their schools, a favourite form of benefaction being improved or increased facilities for games. They were also jealous guardians of the sporting reputations of the schools, strongly deprecating any lowering of former standards and exerting strongly conservative influences against innovations. Teams organised by old boys, such as the Uppingham Rovers and the Old Leysian Rugby Football Club, performed a most valuable function in advertising the sporting prowess of schools and indeed in raising their status. The activities of these clubs were reported exhaustively in the school magazines, while club membership was held out to the boys as the crowning pinnacle of a sporting career at school. A good example of old-boy influence being exerted to resist change occurs at The Leys School in the 1920s when the rising standard of hockey seemed to be endangering the standard of rugby football in the school and the future of the Old Leysian Club. The debt owed by the school to the fame of the club was emphasised, as was the supremacy of the handling game, by old boys, who made bitter attacks upon the supporters of hockey.

The linking of games with the standing and status of the schools is another important factor. This was the reason for Thring's acceptance of a resident professional, for he wrote, '. . . not to have one has become equivalent to losing rank as a school'.[21] This was the reason why the aspiring schools sought to gain fixtures with the established schools, and why such store was set upon the annual MCC game and a fixture at Lord's, the game's headquarters. The concern for comparative status lent itself to snobbery, seen especially in the scramble for fixtures. There was good precedent for the rejection of requests from 'upstarts'. Westminster snubbed Charterhouse and Shrewsbury in turn; a challenge from Mill Hill to Harrow was stated to have brought the reply, 'Eton we know, and Rugby we know, but who are ye?'[22] From Uppingham comes the bitter comment that 'perhaps if we showed Rugby that we could play a little, they might another year think more seriously of playing "a school of our standing" as they are pleased to designate us'.[23] This concern for maintaining and acquiring status was found throughout the range of schools, and was still evident in the scramble for fixtures with public schools by the local-authority grammar schools in the 1920s and 30s.

3

Resistance and reaction

What was in theory play, *and as play most useful and excellent, became the first and most enthralling* business.

George Moberly, 1854, quoted in
J. D'E. E. Firth, *Winchester College,* 139

'Conform or be kicked' is the command written over the portals of every school.

Alfred Lunn, *The Harrovians* (1913)

RESISTANCE TO ATHLETICISM IN THE SCHOOLS

The growth of athleticism was not unchallenged. Dr George Moberly, headmaster of Winchester 1836–66, was perhaps the most eminent antagonist of the raising of the status of inter-school matches. He opposed matches organised by the boys themselves and played at Lords in the holidays, for the boys were unsupervised, and drinking, betting and unruly behaviour resulted. These matches were discontinued in 1854 but four years later the Eton *v* Harrow fixture was renewed, becoming the major school match of the year. Old Wykehamists, intensely indignant at their omission, formed a committee to bring pressure on Moberly to change his mind. Their secretary, Frederick Gale, even circularised 'our gallant fellows in Lucknow and Cawnpore' to support the campaign. Moberly was contemptuous, regarding as 'the merest fancy' the notion that the prestige of Winchester was in any way dependent upon cricket. He objected to the expense, glamour and publicity of the Lord's matches because in the boys' minds '. . . recreation and important duty changed places. What was in theory *play*, and as play most useful and excellent, became the first and most enthralling *business*.'[1] Moberly stood his ground and incurred great unpopularity for doing so; his successor, Ridding, reversed his policy.

The extent and importance of games at Uppingham, particularly cricket, had grown so remarkably by the 1860s that Edward Thring began to resist developments required by the sportsmen. In 1868 he even preached a sermon on the text 'For He hath no pleasure in the strength of a horse, neither delighteth He in any man's legs', in which he warned boys of the dangers of their hero-worship of members of teams and their consequent neglect of their schoolwork! He resisted stubbornly the appointment of a full-time professional cricket coach, but eventually gave way because he was warned that the status of his school would suffer. Over-borne by the cricketers, Thring was adamant that comparable developments should not take place in the school football. He had himself drawn up the rules of the Uppingham game, which was restricted necessarily to house matches and matches against old boys. When the Rugby Football Union was founded in 1871 most schools gave up their individual versions of the game in order to play inter-school matches. Thring would tolerate no discussion of the benefits of a change, though it was made clear that boys going on to the universities felt they were at a disadvantage there. Nor would he allow clothes to be changed from flannels to knickerbockers and stockings, which had become usual else-where by this time, insisting that this was a matter for his juris-diction, not the affair of the games committee. He sought alterna-tives to team games, trying to stress athletic sports, gymnastics and swimming to combat the boys' intense enthusiasm, but with little success. He feared the setting up of a 'rival power' in the school by the athletes, and consequently asserted his authority by punishing rigorously even the most senior athletes when they broke school rules. A schoolboy recorded in 1886 that 'Drabble and Whitwell both in XV and Whitwell captain of the XI had their colours taken away and 10 each for going to the Flower

Show yesterday; changed on their way to football: is an awful shame, especially the licking part.'[2]

As games grew in importance in the 1860s and 70s, becoming more strictly organised and compulsory, it required a headmaster of great personal stature to prevent over-emphasis. Frederick Temple, headmaster of Rugby 1857–69, and himself active physically, had such authority that he was able to initiate reforms in the method of play, such as the abolition of 'keeping goal' (small boys being used simply to return the ball to the field of play), and deliberate hacking, despite the vociferous objections of intensely conservative old boys. He would not allow games to be exalted to the detriment of other aspects of school life, nor would he allow the athletes to assume an authority which would challenge the status of the sixth form. Under succeeding heads who were weaker, the balance he created was lost.[3]

Dr Weymouth, in his inaugural address at Mill Hill School in 1869, called for a sensible middle course in physical education, seeing sport as an essential part of a 'complete and generous education' but stating also that there were dangers associated with excess. Dr Weymouth was a stern disciplinarian and efficient administrator, under whose guidance many academic successes were achieved. Towards the end of his headmastership there was a decline in numbers, attributed by the school's historian in part to competition from the growing grammar schools in the north. He also adds deprecatingly, 'There was much in Dr Weymouth . . . of the best private school rather than of the public school type.' The writer's own sympathy with games is evident in the large amount of space he devotes to recording them.[4] Amongst assistant masters, Oscar Browning's opposition to athleticism in his evidence to the Clarendon Commission has been noted (page 19). In 1875 he was dismissed from his housemaster's position at Eton on the grounds that he had exceeded the number of boys allowed in his house, but some think that it was probably his bitter opposition to athleticism more than any one other factor that caused his dismissal.[5] Lack of co-operation in games was cited in 1867 as a reason for the dismissal of an assistant master at Norwich School. Assistant masters who opposed current policies were evidently wise to keep their views to themselves.

By the last decades of the century it took a very strong personality, even in a headmaster, to effect changes in the established practices of the public schools. A successful example was F. W. Sanderson, who after a highly successful career as head of science and engineering became headmaster of Oundle 1892–1922. Sanderson was faced with a long and fierce struggle against boys, masters and the neighbourhood before he could accomplish the sweeping and fundamental changes he wanted. He stressed the importance of science because this field of knowledge was neglected in the schools, and he wished to bring not only science but the scientific spirit, outlook and methods to Oundle, at the same time enlarging the range of other subjects, including modern languages and basing their study upon the resources of a well-stocked library. Each boy should develop his capacity to the utmost, and Sanderson developed practical subjects, established engineering workshops and made over a hundred acres to agriculture. He wished every boy to take an active part in games, speaking with some scorn of time spent in watching others play, and regretting his own lack of knowledge of games, but was strongly opposed to athletes acquiring undue status or privilege. Sanderson's work was not imitated directly but his success at Oundle made others see there could be variants of the orthodox, constrictive scheme.[6]

Another headmaster with original ideas was G. W. S. Howson, who was appointed to Gresham's School, Holt, in 1900 after being a science master at Uppingham since 1886.[7] Gresham's School benefited from a vast increase of income as the result of the renewal of leases, so that Howson was given the authority and the opportunity to establish his own ideas in what was a virtual refoundation of the school. Because he opposed the supremacy of classics, he excluded Greek from the curriculum. He was also a bitter opponent of athleticism, and took positive measures to ensure that games acquired no undue importance. He not only discouraged sporting papers and publications in the school, but deprecated conversations about sport. He forbade cups and trophies and the playing of inter-school matches. To discourage any suggestion of a professional approach to games he banned both the starter's pistol and the scrum cap. Spectators were allowed to clap, but not to cheer, at matches. In 1912 he announced proudly, 'We declined to build an altar to the god of athletics, preferring him as a servant.' To provide adequate opportunities for exercise Howson gave gymnastics an unusually prominent place, provided open and covered swimming baths, gave an important role to the corps, and established a scout troop at an early date. The boys also had great freedom to wander in the open countryside nearby, and Howson abolished irksome restrictions on doing this on Sundays. His impact was such that his policies were continued after his death in 1919 by his successor, so that inter-school matches were not resumed until the 1930s.

There were a number of opponents of the growth of sport at the universities too. In 1868 Mark Pattison, Rector of Lincoln College, Oxford 1861–84, attacked the 10 per cent of students at Oxford who were so idle that they 'cannot be considered to be nominally pursuing any course of university studies at all'. Indeed such was the concentration on cricket and boating in the summer that he judged the only answer was to end residence in May! Pattison appealed to parents and schoolmasters to effect reform before boys came to the university. He bewailed that games

... have ceased to be amusements: they are organised into a system of serious occupation. What we call incapacity in a young man is often no more than an incapacity of attention to learning, because the mind is pre-occupied with a more urgent and all-absorbing call on its energies. As soon as the summer weather sets in, the colleges are disorganised; study, even the pretence of it, is at an end. Play is thenceforward the only thought. They are playing all day, or preparing for it, or refreshing themselves after their fatigues.[8]

The total influence of the few who resisted athleticism was small, since the established standards of the public school were so deeply entrenched. There was little support for change before 1914, for it seemed to patriotic Englishmen that the schools were geared to produce just those obedient men-of-action the nation needed.

ATHLETICISM IN CONTEMPORARY LITERATURE

A general criticism of athleticism was that it resulted in a denigration of intellectual development. This was one of the major points of Fitzjames Stephen's review of *Tom Brown's Schooldays* in the issue of *Edinburgh* of January 1868. He found the real answer to Arnold's fears of moral childishness to be the encouragement of a variety of ways of stimulating the intellect. This opinion was reiterated by Edward Lyttelton in 1880, and he advocated as a solution less concentration in the schools on the academically gifted and the stimulation of voluntary intellectual effort by the teaching of science, the construction of workshops for manual work, the use of museums and the utilising of school journals for literary and scholarly work.[9]

Arnold Lunn pointed out just how much time was spent playing games: '. . . a vigorous House played every weekday throughout the term . . . in an ordinary term there were some 60 house games and 10 team matches'. He shows how the tyranny of the 'bloods' made games the focus of the life of the house, for while the boy aristocracy was built upon athletic talent, schoolwork was of course low in the accepted scale of values.[10] This theme was returned to by Alec Waugh in 1917 in *The Loom of Youth*, a bitter attack on public schools. Athleticism was 'ruining the country', responsible for the bigoted outlook of the masters and the products of the schools, and the cause of a deep-rooted objection to work amongst the boys. His hero's disillusionment is complete, '. . . for years generation after generation of Fernhurstians had worshipped at the altar of a little tin god. He saw athleticism as it really was, shorn of its glamour, and he knew its poverty.'

Critics pointed out the external forces influencing the schools. Edward Lyttelton wrote of the vast growth of public interest in school games, illustrating his point by comparing the small numbers of spectators at the Eton–Harrow cricket match in the 1850s with its status thirty years later when it was affecting the duration of the London season. The 'motive power' for such developments in the schools was he considered 'the consensus of fashionable public opinion' acting externally upon them. Fundamentally, parental attitudes were at fault, for rarely were habits of study encouraged. H. B. Gray and A. C. Benson agreed that the daily newspapers and periodic journals were responsible for the community's feverish interest in games and the spread of the 'universal contagion' to the schools, Benson stressing the gravity of the result: 'Boys brought up under the influence of an overwhelming preponderance of athletics are apt to lose the balance and proportion of mind and life altogether.'[11]

Many agreed that the masters were responsible in great measure for the developments in the schools. To Lionel Ford the initial benefits were disciplinary, but he blamed masters for not capitalising on the better relationships with the boys.[12] Benson disliked the absorption of masters in games, for he considered their involvement should be paternal rather than partisan and they should have wider interests. Montague blamed masters for presenting the boys with ambivalent attitudes to work; on the one hand they were exhorted, especially in sermons in chapel, to work hard, and on the other they were urged by the games-orientated housemasters and the 'beribboned general' visiting the school to regard success as unrelated to academic endeavour.[13]

The first to attack the theory that sporting activities ensured a high moral code was Wilkie Collins in *Man and Wife* (1870). He dealt with two issues, the 'scandalous state' of the marriage laws and the effects of athleticism. The central figure of the novel, a nobleman's son, is an eminent oarsman and runner, but to Collins those activities were detrimental rather than beneficial to his character development for they 'taught him to take every advan-

tage of another man that his superior strength and superior running can suggest'. Collins views such training with the concomitant neglect of civilising influences as inevitably leading to
disaster.[14] These were unpopular views and do not appear again
for more than thirty years, when in *The Upton Letters* A. C. Benson
connected the low code of morals, the vice and dishonesty of the
public schools with athleticism. In *The Harrovians* Alfred Lunn
showed the effect of these standards in a full portrayal of the lives
of a group of boys, illustrating the misery of house games.
Waugh's *The Loom of Youth*, written when he had just joined the
army from Sherborne School, was a powerful affirmation of the
low behaviour in the schools. 'It's no use trusting a Public School
boy. Put faith in him and he'll take advantage of it.' He contrasted
the boys' own code of behaviour—with its acceptance of immorality, bullying, cheating, and dishonesty—with the official
ethos of the school. The boys' worship of games was all-absorbing
and their values had become so distorted that all that really mat-
tered was the success of the house and the winning of house
competitions, to achieve which any violence was justified. Waugh
felt the school had neither prepared him for life nor for the war:
'GAMES don't win battles, but BRAINS do, and brains aren't
trained on the footer-field.' The irrationality of masters he finds
painfully irritating: 'If you play badly at rugger you are asked
what use you will be in a regiment. If your French prose is full
of howlers, you are told slackers aren't wanted in the trenches.'

Waugh was the first to show the extent of homosexuality in the
schools: the boy who was expelled by the school when his 'vice'
was discovered in fact had the sympathy of his fellows, for they
knew they were equally guilty. The boy himself, justifiably in
Waugh's view, felt a victim of the school, for he had merely
accepted the values of the society he had found there. He had
arrived innocent and was sent away in disgrace, with the bitter
feeling of having been helpless to counter the pressures in boy
society which had led to his involvement. Waugh showed too
that the example was being set by the 'fast bloods', contradicting

the belief widely held by schoolmasters that vigorous exercise was the antidote to 'immorality'. This point of view had been challenged by Edward Lyttelton in 1880, while Benson had gone further, by suggesting a positive connection between games and 'physical temptations', stating that 'the almost adoration' with which a boy athlete was regarded was 'of itself a great danger if a boy is prone to sensual faults'. Waugh's exposure implied that these practices were universal in boy society, which was violently denied by defenders of the schools. Robert Graves repeated the charge in *Goodbye to All That* (1929), stating: 'For every one born homosexual there are at least ten permanent pseudo-homosexuals made by the public school system.' At Charterhouse in his day the chief interests had been games and romantic friendships; schoolwork was despised by everyone.

E. C. Mack was the first to suggest that the growth of organised games originated homosexuality in the schools, because it meant the loss of freedom which the boys had hitherto enjoyed, and this view is supported by T. C. Worsley.[15] But the theory is refuted by evidence of homosexuality in the schools before the 1880s, such as that provided by Sir Geoffrey Faber who quotes Benjamin Jowett's letter written in 1860 to his young second cousin Sidney Irwin. It seems that Jowett's warning was based upon his own experiences at St Paul's in the 1830s. Faber concludes, 'Boys were boys, the tree of knowledge equally tempting, before as after the advent of organised games.'[16]

Criticism of the rule of 'the Bloods' was widespread. Edward Lyttelton stated that in any clash of authority with the prefects the allegiance of the main body of the school was to the athletes, and pointed out further that athletic prowess was no suitable criterion for the choice of those permitted to wield unlimited authority. The extent of this authority was testified to by G. W. Lyttelton: 'In the eyes of the school at large, the chief performers at games can do, or say, no wrong—their position is more absolute than the Pope's and from their decision there is no appeal.'[17] Alfred Lunn, in *The Harrovians*, showed that for the younger boys it meant being sworn at and driven on in house practices and games, and being beaten afterwards if they did not achieve the required result. The eminent position of the athletes was reinforced everywhere by dress, colours and a multitude of trivial customs. At Charterhouse:

> The Bloods of the Eleven ruled the school and dictated school customs. Only in your second term could you wear a knitted tie, only in your second year coloured socks, only in your third year a turned down collar, and only bloods could blossom into light grey trousers and butterfly collars and walk arm-in-arm across the sacred grass. The Sixth had no such privileges . . .[18]

. . . and did not dare to claim them until some of them had become proficient boxers. Robert Graves also began boxing 'seriously and savagely' in order to be left alone by the bloods.

The pressures towards conformity, the constrictive nature of the education and the loss of leisure were seen by the critics to combine to produce a stereotype. Fitzjames Stephen had foreseen that games, by ending the freedom found in the old schools, would effectively destroy self-reliance. Fifty years later Lunn wrote, ' "Conform or be kicked" is the command written over the portals of every school.' So restricted was the boys' outlook that even a mountaineer of the eminence of George Mallory was 'generally despised' because he was neither a disciplinarian nor interested in cricket or football. C. E. Montague and H. G. Wells denounced the preparatory schools for the same sense of values. In *Joan and Peter*, H. G. Wells described the bleak curriculum and the lack of intellectual stimulation in such schools, with the excessive regard paid to games which the boys played 'desperately and excessively because they had nothing better to do'. Even the best of such schools influenced boys so that their resulting 'outlook on the world [was] as broad and as high as the outlook of a bricklayer's labourer'.

The traditional claims that the schools were orientated towards service—to the house, school and nation—were also attacked by the critics. In *Stalky and Co*, Rudyard Kipling attacked the current belief that *esprit de corps* and compulsory games were suitable means of training efficient soldiers and imperial servants. What he praised in the public schools was the code of conduct developed by the boys themselves. Boys who pitted their wits against the authorities learned courage and cunning and knew how to take a beating with disdain if caught. This he saw as the basis of future efficiency: he wrote of such boys, 'They were learning at the expense of a fellow countryman, the lesson of their race, which is to put away all emotion and entrap the alien at the proper time.'

In Kipling's view games were of no value, but his heroes joined the Natural History Society in order to get into the countryside to hunt and to poach, activities which had been common before the advent of organised team games! He returned to this theme after the 'disgrace' of the Boer War and wrote that 'the flannelled fools at the wicket or the muddied oafs at the goals' ought to be preparing themselves realistically to fight for their homeland and empire.[19] Worsley thought the training of the public school boy had been purposeful until the Boer War but completely out of date afterwards. In the 1914–18 war the public school officers earned high praise for their endurance, physical courage and leadership, but in the *Barbarians and Philistines* he wrote that

> . . . the narrowness of intellectual training, the lack of knowledge of technique, the inflexibilities of temperament and lack of imagination, the rigidity of an out-of-date discipline (yours not to reason why), all combined to prolong the war and to increase the casualties very considerably.

Robert Graves observed wryly, 'There was no patriotism in the trenches. It was too remote a sentiment, and rejected as fit only for civilians.'

In estimating the validity of these views it must be remembered that there were variations in the extent of athleticism in the range of schools and in degree also. What in fact the criticisms of games, their status and associated abuses do reveal is the barrenness of the education provided by the schools. As Martin Browne wrote, the fault lay in 'the lack of more important things'; where were the 'new and bigger ideals to push out the old, small ones?'[20] Certainly the criticisms caused no revolutionary changes in the attitudes to games in the schools. Aspects of athleticism, such as compulsory and excessive participation in games were not modified in many schools until after 1945, some day schools making games compulsory even after this. In the vast majority of schools a more tolerant attitude was adopted towards other activities, and a great variety of pastimes were introduced gradually. The public schools were influenced by the growth of the 'progressive' schools and indeed two of the new public schools founded in the 1920s, Rendcomb and Bryanston, adopted many 'progressive' features.

OTHER INFLUENCES UPON THE SCHOOLS

It is interesting to attempt to isolate and evaluate a number of influences which affected developments in the public schools and the state-supported secondary schools. External social agencies, developments within education in general, and developments within physical education in particular, all had repercussions.

In the last quarter of the nineteenth century the military connection was of course very important in the public schools. The establishment of units of the Volunteer Corps had meant the appointment of drill instructors; to these were added physical-training instructors, who taught not only gymnastics but also a range of minor sports such as single-stick, boxing, fencing, swimming and shooting. Until the 1930s there was no source of trained men in England other than the army or navy. Establishments varied according to the amount of interest taken and according to the wealth of the particular school. At Harrow from 1935–40 there was a Director of Physical Education—Captain A. D. F. Thomason—a full-time remedial gymnast and six instructors, who covered gymnastics and minor sports (but not rackets, squash or fives) as well as all the OTC work for the 400 boys.[21] Some schools on the other hand, had only one instructor, who combined drilling the corps with teaching some gymnastics. An even cheaper method of teaching gymnastics was in the use of senior boys to instruct groups arranged on a house basis.

The foundation of the Naval Physical Training School in 1902 also left an imprint on the schools, for after a number of trials the navy adopted the Swedish system, and courses of training were begun. Unlike the army, the navy used officer-instructors, a number of whom went to Sweden for further training and subsequently took posts in schools.[22] F. M. Grenfell, after instructing at the naval school for five years, served at Eton for two years, leaving in 1909 to become one of Sir George Newman's inspectors at the Board of Education. Similar appointments led to the establishment of the Swedish system in a small number of schools. The appointment of ex-officers meant raising the status of physical training for it was now in the charge of men equal in social status to other masters. The army also adopted the Swedish system in 1907, but the boys retained their traditional disdain of such activities, for example, the 'new prominence' given to physical training at Rugby in 1911 was far from popular.[23] Gymnastics was still organised quite independently from games, its relatively unimportant position remaining unchanged.

Most of these instructors returned to the forces at the outbreak of war in 1914, but the close links between the services and the schools were re-established after the war. Officers usually attended a special course at Aldershot before taking up their school appointments. The army prized its links with the schools, a number of direct-grant and grammar schools as well as public schools, for a number of reasons, one being to preserve an avenue of congenial employment for NCOs when their period of service expired. Such employment continued happily until the mid-1930s when it became apparent that these instructors were of an inferior calibre to properly trained physical-education masters. However, the supply of such teachers was very limited until the foundation of Carnegie College in 1933. Additional courses were established at Loughborough in 1935 and at Goldsmiths' College in 1937. A three-year course was also established at Loughborough at the

School of Athletics, specifically to train specialist staff for the public schools. However, as no subjects other than physical education were studied, those who completed the course did not gain recognition as trained teachers. For this reason, and because of students' difficulties in obtaining grants, the course was not renewed after World War II.

The acceleration of the supply of specialist teachers after 1945 meant fewer opportunities for ex-service instructors. Those who now serve in the schools are usually limited to a specialised activity, such as swimming or fencing instruction. For many years these instructors have made an important contribution to the teaching of gymnastics and minor sports, sometimes coaching boys to a high standard of performance. In some respects, however, they may have held back the development of physical education, for their inferior social position and limited education reflected adversely upon the activities they taught, while their training and experience militated against experimentation and innovation in teaching methods and in the range of sports.

The broadening of physical education to include such outdoor pursuits as camping, tracking and associated activities can be traced to the influence of the para-military youth organisations, planned and organised originally for working-class boys, but developing rapidly to include the sons and daughters of the middle classes and to influence the schools. Industrialised working boys were denied the opportunity of playing games and of exercise in the open air. A miner's son began to work underground at twelve years of age, and for a large portion of the year he could be going to work and returning home in darkness. In all industrial towns and cities there was an almost total lack of facilities for the recreation of working-class children. Camping holidays and certain weekend activities were begun by one London boys' club in the late 1870s, and were being sponsored by the Boys Brigade and a boys' club in Manchester in the mid-1880s. During these years individual teachers were struggling against difficulties to organise team games in the board schools, in the main using public parks for their playing fields, while from the late seventies university and public-school men brought games to working boys.[24] Military drill and exercises were also introduced to some of the boys' clubs with ex-NCO instructors in charge. Outdoor activities were developed by the Boys Brigade (founded by William Smith in Glasgow in 1883), whose formula of Bible class and 'manly' pastimes, linked with arms drill, a simple uniform and a flute band, achieved great success. The first camp was held in 1886; ten years later hundreds of camps were organised.[25] At the anniversary parade in Glasgow in 1905, Baden-Powell suggested that greater variety in training would be beneficial, and after some experimental work with boys he published his *Handbook for Scouts* in 1908.

The ideas expressed in this work were so well received that although it was originally intended for existing organisations it generated the Boy Scout movement. Practical scouting was offered as an alternative to watching games, though again the stress was upon character development. The military connection was strong, for not only was Major-General Baden-Powell the founder but other high-ranking officers had official roles in the movement. Lord Haldane expressed his opinion to Baden-Powell in the following terms: 'I feel the organisation of the Boy Scouts has so important a bearing on the future that probably the greatest service you can render the country is to devote yourself to it.'[26] The movement appealed because it combined a para-military patriotism with a return to the outdoors. By 1913 there were nearly 14,000 scouts in Great Britain, and there was rapid growth overseas. Baden-Powell was keen to use the movement as a means of social progress among poor boys in the slums, but seeing the need also for leaders of high calibre wished to found troops in the public schools, though most of these held aloof until after 1918. Troops were formed in many of the old grammar schools in the early years; some preparatory schools followed suit, while the progressive schools were enthusiastic supporters. The movement continued to grow (despite a decline of membership, especially of the older boys, in the 1930s), reaching 47,000 members in 1945. Its reputation was increased by the tradition of community service, particularly during the two world wars.[27]

By spreading interest in outdoor pastimes the scout movement has had an important influence upon the development of physical education. In a number of the public schools scouting became accepted as an alternative to the corps, but its major support has been from middle-class and working-class boys. Originally Haldane wished to see scouting as a stage preparatory to military training, but scouts seem to have developed scouting for its own sake rather than as part of a national plan of military preparedness. By reviving and developing interest in the countryside the scout movement helped to ensure an enthusiastic reception for later ideas for developing outdoor pursuits as an alternative or supplement to team games. The movement itself has been susceptible to change, and has over the years broadened the scope of its activities and accepted eagerly the methods of such innovators as Kurt Hahn.

The progressive schools also influenced the development of physical education. Founded to provide an alternative kind of education for upper-class children, they catered especially for the progeny of the 'liberal intelligentsia'.[28] Such schools were individualistic in many respects, varying according to the character and educational aims of their particular founders. Of their many common features, one was the rejection of athleticism and the relegation, to a greater or lesser degree, of team games. Cecil Reddie, the founder of Abbotsholme School in 1889, and the first of a new wave of innovators, vehemently opposed the excesses associated with games, deploring the constricting effect upon the boys. The progressive schools also showed a deeper concern for the physical health and hygiene of their pupils. Reddie seems to have been influenced by H. H. Almond's work at Loretto Academy in Scotland; certainly they had a common concern for wholesome diet, the abolition of 'tuck', a simple form of clothing and stress upon personal hygiene. J. H. Badley, the founder of Bedales School, deplored the disregard of hygiene in the public schools in his day, when boys had only one bath a week though they played games daily. He gave gymnastics a much more important role, stressing the value of complete and harmonious physical development and remedial exercises to deal with defects associated with physical growth. He advocated the adoption of the Swedish system, appointing R. E. Roper, a classics graduate who had spent two years studying at the Central Gymnastics Institute in Stockholm, to take charge of the physical education at his school in 1913. A similar concern for physical development was shown by Alexander Devine, who introduced a Spartan regime at Clayesmore, and at the King Alfred School Society's 'Rational' School at Hampstead.

Although this very small group of progressive schools in existence before the formation of the Board of Education and the local education authorities were associated with an idealistic socialism, the fees they charged meant that they did not accept working-class children; indeed their only direct contact with the working class seems to have been Devine's invitation to groups of working men to spend Sunday afternoons and evenings with him and his boys at Clayesmore. Their importance in physical education is that they illustrate existence of an alternative to the traditional pattern, and that they set new standards of provision for the healthy development and hygiene of their pupils.

Other older foundations with many similar features became merged with the 'new' schools noted above in the progressive schools movement in 1914. Perhaps the most important group was that of Quaker schools, comprising nine founded in the period 1808–42, and Leighton Park established as a Quaker public school in 1890. From early years Friends included exercise in their schools, walking and manual work being the usual forms of organised activity, while the children had their own unorganised games. Organised team games, when they came later, were never allowed an undue importance. Rough games were not allowed— John Ford, head of Bootham School in Yorkshire, introduced football after a visit to Rugby, but modified the rules to make it more gentle—and nor was competitive athletics. In the present century, games and physical-education activities grew in importance, but were always seen as just part of a wide range of school activities and did not acquire undue prominence.[29] After 1918 the mood of disenchantment encouraged a wide variety of new foundations, with the emphasis upon co-education, children's freedom and self-government, and the predominance of emotional development. There was an absolute rejection of the exaltation of games, as J. H. Whitehouse, the founder of Bembridge School on the Isle of Wight typifies.

Perhaps the most radical of the new establishments was A. S. Neill's at Summerhill in Suffolk, but in physical education the most interesting was Bryanston in Dorset, opened in 1928. Here schoolwork was based on the Dalton Plan, founded on an organised scheme of private study, while in physical education a compromise between the permissiveness of the more radical progressive schools and the compulsion of the orthodox public schools was achieved. All boys played games in their first three years, then were free to choose from a range of the more individual sports such as climbing and canoeing. As a preferred alternative to the OTC, the Pioneers were formed in 1933 to provide an opportunity for constructive work in community projects. Pioneer holidays included expeditions for exploration, and periods spent at Outward Bound sea and mountain schools. In its breadth of approach and sponsoring of a wide variety of activities, Bryanston anticipated by many years what has since become an orthodox pattern of physical education.

The greatest impetus for the development of outdoor activities came, however, from Gordonstoun School in Scotland, founded by Kurt Hahn in 1934.[30] Hahn's platonic theories of education had been developed at the Schule Schloss Salem founded by Prince Max of Baden in 1920. Here a high priority was originally given to physical health and fitness because of the malnutrition resulting from the war. The importance attached to character training in Hahn's scheme was highlighted by the original divisions of staff, the 'character-training staff' and the 'academic staff'. Hahn made physical activities compulsory and organised, so as to foster self-discipline. Expedition work was a prominent feature; every boy was to learn a craft and to sail a boat, almost all acted, all ran, jumped and threw, all the year round. Games were merely one of a number of physical activities, being given no more importance than seamanship, fire-fighting, estate work, and other activities. Service to the community was stressed by building a coastguard hut, and by manning a coastguard service and a fire service. Later these services were extended to include mountain rescue, surf rescue and a ski patrol. Each boy was responsible for his own physical fitness, keeping his own training plan, which was supervised during the first two years and then entirely his own matter. Hahn publicised his methods in broadcasts and written articles, and by the success of his pupils in the public schools athletics meetings between 1933 and 1938. He gained most notice, however, from his initiation of the Moray Badge, which developed into the County Badge Scheme and was the predecessor of the Duke of Edinburgh's Award Scheme. The Moray Badge (based upon the German sports badge), was earned by fitness tests, completing expeditions and passing life-saving tests.

The years of World War II gave a wider currency to Hahn's ideas. The boys of Gordonstoun were evacuated to Wales, where in 1940 a summer school for young soldiers and public-school boys was held to demonstrate his methods. In 1941 the Outward Bound Sea School was established to provide four-week courses of pre-service training, the Outward Bound Trust being founded in 1946. By the end of the 1950s four Trust schools were providing courses for youths from all walks of life. The courses were physically rigorous and demanding, but above all based upon Hahn's theories of character development from experience gained on mountains or the sea. These ideas have been adopted by a number of overseas schools and when the Atlantic College in Glamorgan was founded in 1962 its physical education was a copy of work at Gordonstoun.

Hahn's work has its critics, but certainly his ideas have permeated physical education. Outdoor activities are now an integral part of the programmes in both public and local-authority schools. Outdoor-activity centres, in the mountains or near the sea, have multiplied. Many agree with Hahn that expeditions are fine agencies for character development, while others are concerned rather with the acquisition of skills providing an immediate interest, and also in many cases introducing recreations enjoyed throughout adult life, as well as providing the immediate and later benefits of exercise in the open air. This growth of outdoor activities owes a great deal to their high regard at Gordonstoun and the subsequent dissemination of ideas from there.[31]

Another external influence which has affected the development of physical education is that of the medical profession. Dr Clement Dukes, the medical officer of Rugby School, was an early propagandist for the improvement of living conditions to ensure the fitness and good health of schoolboys. Other doctors showed interest in the subject and offered a diversity of opinions, ranging from Sir James Paget's preference for the national games as a means of physical development to John Holm's rejection of the value of all activities other than Ling's gymnastics.[32] The establishment of the School Medical Service in 1907 brought persistent official encouragement for the adoption of the Swedish system in the secondary schools. The Board of Education suggested standards for gymnasiums, for the official stress was upon the corrective and developmental value of exercise. Progress was slow, because trained teachers were so scarce that many schools employed ex-service instructors, because suitable gymnasiums were slow to appear, and above all because the schools preferred the traditional games to gymnastic exercise.

Medical influence also affected the way in which physical activities were taught. The basic concern of Swedish work was postural. As R. E. Roper wrote, 'The work of one responsible for physical education in a school is to all intents and purposes a living sculpture, a modelling of bodies.' During wartime a more widespread interest in posture had grown from the work of various establishments in industry—out of which also developed the new subject of industrial psychology.[33] This interest in posture continued in the 1920s, until it became the accepted criterion for the evaluation of physical education in schools.[34]

To remedy the shortage of teachers of gymnastics the Board of Education organised vacation courses from 1924. A number of masters on the first course joined together to form the Secondary Schoolmasters' Physical Education Association, later joined by a small group of masters working in public schools. Links were established with leaders in medicine, among them Lord Dawson of Penn and Sir Alfred Fripp, who became powerful advocates of a more broadly based physical education. The association was joined by a number of doctors, F. E. Friend and F. W. W. Griffin making notable contributions in the 1930s.

A further link was established with the medical profession in 1935 when, at the instigation of the Minister of Health, the British Medical Association set up a Physical Education Committee to assess means of 'raising national standards of physical efficiency'. The report of the committee revealed the inadequacy of the provision for physical education in the schools: the lack of equipment and playing fields in the state schools, the lack of qualified masters to teach physical education in the secondary and public schools and the neglect of gymnastics because of the preference for games. The committee came down heavily on the side of gymnastic exercises, showing the government clearly what measures were needed to effect improvements both for those at school and for the neglected post-school adolescents. By stressing the value of the combined work of doctors and teachers of physical education in preventive medicine and in creating 'greater health, fitness and happiness for the people as a whole', the committee helped to raise the status of those engaged in this work in schools.

Within physical education individuals laboured to spread the gospel and to establish the work upon soundly based scientific principles. Madame Bergman-Osterberg changed profoundly the character of physical education for girls, initially by her work in the London elementary schools, later by making the teaching of the subject a suitable career for middle-class girls.[35] Her college was established some fifty years before a comparable means of training men teachers existed. Other colleges were established and the Ling Physical Education Association was founded to spread the work. The influence of officers trained in Swedish gymnastics while in the navy has already been noted. To them must be added a pacifist, R. E. Roper, who after a short period at Eton took over physical education at Bedales School. Roper considered that gymnastic training alone could combat successfully the results of the lengthy sitting, still enforced on schoolchildren—such as decreased vitality, a lessened mobility of the chest, lack of tone in the abdominal muscles, nervous strain and eyestrain. Gymnastics —using the essential Swedish apparatus of wallbars, ropes and beams, horse and box—were imperative for a minimum of three half-hour periods a week. Accurate records of growth and remedial classes for the 30 per cent in need of special treatment were also essential. To establish the work in schools, Roper wished to raise the status of his subject by the use of scientific experiments and by the creation of university courses to meet the urgent need for specialist training. He was an important innovator in many respects, pioneering work in tests and measurements and influencing directly a group of teachers who worked on lines he advocated. Among his students were P. A. Smithells, G. W. Hedley and G. W. Murray, who established physical education departments at Gresham's School, Mill Hill and Queen Elizabeth's, Barnet, respectively. Murray defined the new concept of the subject:

> In its widest interpretation Physical Education embraces all the physical activities in which boys take part, together with periodic weighing and measuring and examination of physique. It includes some study of change in normal and abnormal growth and development, and it should work in close connection with the school doctor. In addition, it is essential that there should be a

close link with the academic side of education, and it requires the friendly co-operation of the headmaster, housemasters, and all others with whom the boys come into contact.[36]

M. L. Jacks, headmaster of Mill Hill at twenty-eight, appointed G. W. Hedley to his staff, for Hedley matched his ideal of a university-trained man of wide interests and sympathies 'whose duty it will be to promote to the highest the physical development of each individual'. Jacks placed great stress upon 'the skill-demanding and skill-producing extra-curricular activities of the school', forecasting that the development of this aspect of schoolwork would be the chief reform in educational practice in the future. His father, L. P. Jacks, was a powerful supporter of physical education, calling in a series of lectures and publications, from 1931 onwards, for a new spirit in education, involving a 'large vision of life as a unitary whole' and the 'education of the whole man'. He viewed man as 'a skill-hungry animal', and condemned the existing education system for not satisfying his needs. He maintained that in addition to the 70 per cent of London elementary schoolchildren known to have remediable physical defects, there was an even higher proportion of 'physical illiterates', cut off from the world of skill by the undisciplined condition of their bodies. He believed

> ... the next great step forward in human education will be in the direction of integrating the education of the body with the education of the mind, bringing the two to the same level of dignity and importance, and making education of that kind accessible to everybody.[37]

The work of the pioneers, reinforced by the encouragement of the propagandists, undoubtedly influenced developments in the 1930s. However, the vast majority of the public schools remained wedded to games as the major instrument of physical education, while the elementary schools were so handicapped that in the earlier part of the decade the usual pattern of work was of free-standing exercises taught in the playground to children wearing unsuitable clothes. Hope for the future was brought by the Hadow Reports which led to the establishment of 'modern' schools equipped with gymnasiums. Many grammar schools had a gymnasium, or at least a hall equipped for gymnastics, but lacked specialist teachers. The Carnegie College at Leeds was opened in 1933 as the result of a grant from the charitable trust. Government action followed in 1935 and while this was not mainly inspired by educational motives, the quality and type of work was influenced directly by the philosophy and achievements of the pioneers. Advances, however, were made on a broad front; the universities were influenced, appointing lecturers in physical education to the training departments, and several provincial universities appointed directors of physical education to sponsor and develop activities amongst the student population. Progress, in the schools and elsewhere, was held up during World War II. These years also brought new ideas to challenge the Swedish and therapeutic basis of gymnastics and the wide development of extra-curricular activities became an important feature of the post-war years.

4

Physical education in the elementary schools 1800–70

No single power of the human body . . . is ever for one moment from under the influences of the others.

David Stow, *The Training System*
(1845), 49–50

This exercise [drill], properly administered, will greatly contribute to the health and spirits of the boys, give them an erect and proper form, and habits of attention, celerity and order.

Robert Owen, *A New View of Society*
(1816)

During the period 1800–70 two major influences shaping the development of physical activities in the elementary schools may be discerned. Firstly, there were those educational theorists and practitioners who followed the concept of the education of the whole person as expressed by Rousseau. As Rousseau had stressed the social training gained by participating in games and physical activities, and their moral value, so they too advocated the necessity of physical activity for individual development. Emphasising the unity of the individual personality they rejected the separation of intellectual aspects from moral and physical aspects of the child's growth. This led to a wider conception of education than that implicit in the monitorial system with its mechanical drilling of the basic skills of literacy, to the inclusion of music, movement and play, and to an insistence upon the necessity of playgrounds. Secondly, there were those who saw physical drill as a means of instilling a basic discipline in the schools. Some saw 'breaks' of

72

drill as assuring the attentiveness of children to their lessons, others as a relief from the monotony of classwork. At its most limited drill was confined to marching children in and out of school in an orderly manner, or to the stretching of limbs while still in their desks. At its most ambitious it became para-military in character, patriotic teachers regarding it as preparing their charges for future service to the nation.

Rousseau's ideas were disseminated in two main ways: by the writing of English educationists and their continental counterparts, and by the imitation of methods used in the schools of continental pioneers, especially when restrictions on travel were removed after 1815. First in the former category were Thomas Day and R. L. Edgeworth; the practical experiments of both of them in bringing up children on the principles of Émile's education have been described many times. In *Sandford and Merton*, Day rejected the values of aristocratic society and the values and methods of conventional schools based upon the requirements of that society. To him, education was important chiefly for its moral influence, for it was the decisive formative influence upon character; moreover, he saw a wide range of experience as necessary for the full development of a complete individual. Edgeworth was pleased with the physical results of the training of his son according to Rousseau's tenets: 'uncommon strength and hardiness of body, great vivacity . . . Whatever regarded the health and strength and agility of my son had amply justified the system of my master.'[1] Other less pleasing features such as the boy's disobedience, however, lead him to abandon the experiment. With his daughter Maria he wrote *Practical Education*, a very full account of their methods of teaching children, based upon their experiences with his own brood of nineteen children. Generally they advocated the use of scientific methods; thus in learning physical skills they suggested an experimental approach. They valued exercise as a means of relieving tension, finding dancing 'an agreeable exercise useful to the health, and advantageous, as it confers a certain degree of habitual ease and grace'. They wished physical activities to comply with two general principles—to be pleasurable and to bring the joy of success.

Another supporter of a liberal programme of physical activities in schools at this time was Erasmus Darwin, famous as the author of a compendious medical work, *Zoonomia*. Darwin maintained that education should contain a balance of academic work and physical activity, and though in *Female Education* he expressed his deprecation of those schools for girls which devoted too much time to music and dancing, yet he was convinced that the lives of young people were too sedentary. He recommended that some hours each day should be spent at bodily exercises, play and dancing. The importance of these writers lies in their influence upon later innovators establishing schools on a larger scale than those of the Edgeworths or of Darwin's daughters. Robert Owen, for example, would have known of these theories through his membership of the Literary & Philosophical Society in Manchester in the 1790s.

Owen's schools at New Lanark in Scotland have been described many times.[2] Their interest here is in the importance given to physical activities by Owen, and because in effect he combined the two major influences previously described, giving physical education the role advocated by innovating educators, but also including a strong element of drilling and marching. Owen also saw education as the great agency for moulding character and wanted a national system of education for the poor based upon the creation of a 'well-trained, united and happy people'. It was his concern for the quality of education that made him reject out of hand the mechanical teaching of the skills of literacy by the monitorial systems of Bell and Lancaster; he would have no truck with the 'irrational' basis of their systems. To create happy and healthy individuals, dancing and singing were essential parts of his curriculum. The value of dancing was, he said, 'a pleasant, healthful, natural and social exercise, calculated to improve the carriage and deportment, and to raise the spirits, and increase the cheerfulness and hilarity of those engaged in it'.[3]

74

Owen showed concern for the physical welfare of the pupils throughout their period of education. This began at three, in the infant school, with instruction being combined with activities that would result in active, happy children. When it was fine much time was spent outdoors. In the 'superior' school for children aged from five or six to ten, an hour or two hours each day were devoted to physical work, including dancing. The boys and girls were clad in uniforms—ginghams and kilts—and danced in bare feet to the music of an orchestra. After the age of ten they attended a voluntary school held in the evenings, about 400 attending the two-hour sessions. Here again exercise was included.[4] With the dancing was combined drilling as a means of preparing children for military service, Owen believing that 'even the most rational must, for their personal security, learn the means of defence'. Marching was to lead to firearm drill and the 'more complicated military movements'. Though Owen saw the benefits of drill as better discipline and increased smartness, he was aware of the incipient dangers; so to make the work pleasurable it was done to the accompaniment of a fife-and-drum band and the periods of work were kept short.

In Owen's scheme the playground was accorded an important place as a means of social training, for it was here as well as in the school that children would learn the concern for the happiness and welfare of others which he regarded as a fundamental principle of education. The success of his schools astounded contemporary observers, for it was evident that the children were clean, healthy and happy, that they were adjusted socially and were literate.[5] His theories are an essentially personal amalgam, owing a major debt to earlier educationists. It is possible that his belief in the value of military drill derived from Adam Smith's belief in the degeneration of the labouring poor and the imperative need of a form of military training to ensure higher standards of physical fitness.[6] In the context of the prevalent wholesale poverty, ignorance and squalor, Owen's schools are an amazing innovation in working-class education. His concern for the health and happiness of the children is quite alien to the spirit of charitable efforts in the education of the poor at that time.

Owen's methods were in use at New Lanark for eight years only, for in 1824 his partner William Allen enforced his withdrawal from the management of the schools. Allen opposed Owen's religious unorthodoxy and regarded the music, dancing and drilling as pernicious. Teachers, including the dancing master, were dismissed and the monitorial system introduced. Owen's ideas were, however, carried elsewhere, and became particularly influential in the field of infant education. James Buchanan, who had been appointed by Owen to teach at New Lanark in 1818, left to take charge of an infant school at Westminster, there meeting Samuel Wilderspin and instructing him in his methods. Wilderspin in turn took charge of an infant school at Spitalfields, but attracted most attention as a publicist of the idea of infant schools, and as propagandist.[7] He aided the foundation of schools in London, Kent and Sussex, then acted as travelling agent for the London Infant School Society. Soon he was travelling all over the United Kingdom, lecturing and explaining his system. By 1835 about 300 schools had been founded as the result of his efforts.

Wilderspin adopted and adapted the ideas of Owen and Buchanan in several ways. He regarded the provision of a playground and outdoor training as essential for health and the development of social and moral values. Teachers ought to have oversight of these activities, which should take place in an environment suitable for constructive play. Thus borders for trees and flowers were needed and wooden bricks for building. Rotary swings or 'giant strides' not only provided exercise but also social training. Freedom of choice of activity was essential for character development.[8] These were his ideals, but because so many schools in towns and cities had such cramped quarters that there was no space for exercise, he evolved a type of desk drill, involving such movements as raising hands to counts of a hundred and alternate raising of feet. Not surprisingly he had to warn his readers that they must see that 'graceful' actions were adopted for there was a danger of the proceedings lapsing into buffoonery! The limitations of the physical benefits of such desk drill are obvious.

An example of Wilderspin as a propagandist is shown clearly in Norwich. In 1836 he examined a large number of infants drawn from various schools before a large gathering in St Andrew's Hall. Among other techniques, he illustrated his desk drill, his demonstration being voted a great success despite some trouble from infants who were so small that they kept rolling out of their seats. The demonstration achieved the required result, for a subsequent meeting established the Norfolk & Norwich Infant School Society, which founded St Andrew's Infant School as a model school within a short period. There is no record of the subjects taught here, but a report of one of the new district schools established in the city at St Augustine's in 1838 refers to a 'spacious playground', while a booklet published for the opening states:

> The lower School-room, appropriated to infants between two and seven years of age, can contain about 200 children, who will be taught in the usual amusing manner, blending playfulness with instruction, and communicating to the infant mind early moral and religious principles through means of music, pictures and innocent exercises, both in the school-room and in the playground.

Similarly Wilderspin's influence led to the spread of Owen's ideas in many other parts of the country. Thus in Lancashire, music, movement and play were included in the infant schools. At Salford, 'stress was laid on the playground as a supervised and clean refuge from the streets', while at St Helens physical exercise was obtained by play periods, a 'March to the Gallery' and a crocodile walk for part of one afternoon. In Liverpool, David Goyder was a more direct disciple of Owen and Pestalozzi, the former's influence being evinced by marching for discipline and exercise, and singing 'to calm the turbulent'.[9]

Many other followers of Owen took up aspects of his educational theories and practices, dancing and gymnastics being found in the schools established by radicals such as the Co-operators,

Rational Religionists and Chartists.[10] William Lovett was a firm believer in the value of physical activity and in the need of children to understand the physiological benefits of fresh air and exercise. To encourage this he wrote a textbook, *Elementary Anatomy and Physiology*, which was used in a number of schools.[11] The inclusion of physical education in these schools is indicative of a wider concept of education than that found in the schools of religious societies. Chartist requests for increased educational opportunity were linked with their political programme and with demands for shorter working hours for children.

IMITATION OF CONTINENTAL PRACTICE

Physical education was introduced to various schools in England by those who imitated the practice of continental educationists, for Rousseau's theories had been developed into practical systems of education in which physical education played a major role.[12] J. B. Basedow's work at Dessau is the seminal influence: physical activities were encouraged in a scheme of education which rejected a barren grammarian approach and was based upon learning from actual experience. To gymnastics and long expeditions on foot were added swimming, fencing and horse-riding by J. F. Simon, J. J. du Toit and C. G. Salzmann, the latter including in his programme three hours' exercise daily in the open air.[13] At Schepfenthal, J. C. GutsMuths, by observation and creative experiment, built a complete system of physical education for children; his books, translated into many languages, exerted a widespread influence throughout Europe. Many travellers, however, were influenced directly by the work in Switzerland of Pestalozzi, von Fellenberg and Jacob Werhli.

Pestalozzi made an interesting attempt to analyse physical movements in order to facilitate methods of teaching. His aim was to develop *Fertigkeit*, a word which causes his translator some difficulty, but which is explained as (1) promptitude or readiness, (2) readiness or skill in performing some action. He examined natural actions, such as throwing, turning and swinging, seeking their common factors and so developing an ABC of actions which could be linked with an 'ABC of sense exercises, and with all the mechanical practice in thinking, and with exercise in form and number-teaching'. He advocated a graduated series of such exercises 'from simplest beginning to their highest perfection', but concludes sadly, 'All these as far as popular instruction is concerned are castles in the air.'[14] Pestalozzi's school at Yverdon attracted pupils from all over Europe. Dr Charles Mayo, chaplain at the school from 1819, set up a private boarding school on his return to England. This school included public school games and Pestalozzian exercises in its physical education. Ten minutes were allowed for play at the end of each lesson and an hour given to play between 12.45 and 1.45 pm and between 3.0 and 4.0 pm. But the games played were those of the public schools—football, cricket and fives.[15]

Other English visitors were impressed by the work they saw in Switzerland. Dr Bell wrote of Yverdon and Fellenberg's school at Hofwyl, 'I had almost forgotten the gymnastics which constitute a principal part of the instruction at both these schools and which deserve imitation to a certain degree.'[16] Fellenberg's school, being designed for the sons of gentlemen, was most expensive. Activities in the open air were accorded an important place, for while nine hours a day were spent in study the rest of the time was used in following individual interests which included riding, swimming, dancing and gymnastics.[17] In 1813 Fellenberg brought Werhli to Hofwyl, to develop his school for destitute children and a small training school for teachers. In 1833 Werhli moved to Kreuzlingen to take charge of a new training college, where both gymnastics and gardening were included in the timetable. This college made so deep an impression upon Sir James Kay-Shuttleworth and Carleton Tufnell that they incorporated many of its features in the Normal College opened in Battersea in 1840. Physical training was included:

At seven Drill Instructor Cousens arrives from the Duke of York's school and we go through the marching and extension exercises on one evening and practice on the parallel bars the next. Our directors set much value on these exercises, holding that 'an erect and manly gait, a firm and regular step, precision and rapidity of movement, promptitude in obedience to command, and particularly neatness in apparel and person, insensibly lay the foundation of moral habits and give a practical moral lesson, perhaps more powerful than the precepts which are inculcated by words'.[18]

Gymnastics at Battersea was for the personal benefit of the students, there being no suggestion of its use as a teaching subject in schools.

PUBLIC INTEREST IN GYMNASTICS

Meanwhile gymnastics as a pastime for adults was growing in popularity.[19] GutsMuths' system had been popularised by the publication of his work, and a disciple of his, P. H. Clias, had run courses in military and naval establishments. Works published by Clias and Donald Walker made the German system known. Practitioners of medical gymnastics brought Swedish gymnastics as developed by Ling, to England, while Archibald MacLaren developed his own system, opening a gymnasium and fencing school at Oxford in the 1850s. He influenced the army in particular, the establishment of a gymnasium at Aldershot being followed by others at the major military centres. Provision for civilians was made by the open-air gymnasium on Primrose Hill in 1848 and by the gymnasiums opened later in the large cities. These developments in society were accompanied by some examples of early interest in physical activities in schools for middle-class children. At their Hazelwood School the Hills allocated games, gymnastics and swimming an important role.[20] They had been convinced of the desirability of physical activities by the Rev Lant Carpenter's *Principles of Education: Intellectual, Moral and Physical* published in 1820. The boys played cricket and football, and had an hour each day for athletic sports, which included running, leaping, wrestling, vaulting and spear throwing. Swimming was taught in the school's own pool—which probably influenced the

Rev S. D. Waddy, who became a governor of the Wesleyan Grammar School opened at Sheffield in 1838, which included a 'capacious swimming bath'.[21] At University College School, founded in 1830, gymnastics were being taught 'by a certain Capt Chiosso' as early as 1840.[22]

In the schools provided by the National Society and the British Society, some development of physical activities was encouraged by the inspectors of the Committee of Council on Education, itself set up to supervise the effective use of government grants to the two societies. The Committee's regulations included no stipulation for the provision of playgrounds but such developments were encouraged:

> ... if the master be unprovided with an exercise-ground, he is without the most effectual means of ascertaining, by being a spectator or joining in their sports, the characters of the children under his care, and of training their habits. ... The physical education of the children may therefore be usefully provided for on other grounds than its tendency to develop the muscular powers, and to render the scholars robust and vigorous. The physical exercises of the playground extend the moral influence of the teacher, by encouraging the children to remain under his care during the hours of recreation.[23]

Inspectors were instructed to note the state of the playground and to examine pupil teachers' proficiency in the teaching of exercises. There were so many basic problems to be overcome in the schools that it is doubtful whether such sponsorship of physical activities achieved much success. Two major difficulties were the absence of trained teachers and the paucity of school playgrounds, particularly in the town schools. Some teachers were encouraged to take the children in gymnastic exercises after school hours,[24] but the general picture was bleak, HM Inspector Bellairs regretting in 1884 that 'the old sports of Merrie England had been superseded by the gin shop and beer house. Every village he thought should have its playing field where boys could play after school.'[25]

Physical activities were encouraged also in the schools attached to the newly established institutions for the training of teachers. An important influence was that of David Stow, whose Sunday schools and infant schools in Glasgow had been added to by the establishment of the Glasgow Normal Seminary in 1836. Stow's educational system was eclectic, his debt to Wilderspin's emphasis on physical education being freely admitted.[26] Stow again emphasised the moral purposes of education: 'The playground animates, invigorates, and permits the *steam* which may have accumulated to *escape*, not in furious mischief, but in innocent, joyous and varied amusements, under the superintendence of the master.'[27] Exercises were valued not merely for the physical benefits but also for the cultivation of good habits and obedient behaviour. At Battersea, Kay-Shuttleworth employed tutors from Stow's seminary, and they were recruited also for other training schools, for example at Westminster, which was founded in 1851. Others trained in Glasgow were employed in English schools, the Wesleyans especially recruiting there for a number of years.[28] Stow's and like influences were reflected in the provision made in schools; for example, each of the five schools connected with Westminster College had access to playgrounds, in which four 'giant strides' and a rope climbing-frame were erected.[29]

Unfortunately the ideas of educationists such as Stow became diluted when applied by untrained masters, as the evidence of the assistant commissioner investigating schools in the western counties for the Newcastle Commission indicates:

> The playgrounds attached to the schools are of very slight utility for any purpose of recreation beyond affording a place where the children can be turned out between lessons to get a mouthful of fresh air. A solitary pole for a giant's stride (at the time of my visit, which was in the winter, with the ropes generally missing) is the only feature to indicate that the ground before you is for purposes of play. In one or two places there is a covered shed, nominally for use in wet weather. The games played seemed generally aimless, as though there were no one taking any interest in them or directing them—for good games need to be taught as well as lessons—and I do not think that the encouragement of healthy

athletic sports such as cricket, football etc. has yet found the legitimate place in the education of boys of this class which Public School men would desire, who vividly remember how much it contributed to their own.[30]

RESTRICTIONS IMPOSED BY THE REVISED CODE OF 1862

The Newcastle Commission had been established because the increase of the annual Parliamentary grant to £663,435 in 1858 had engendered a demand for a reduction in expenditure and for a better return for the money spent. The ten assistant commissioners were given no brief to investigate either physical education or playgrounds. To reduce the state grant and make the teaching more effective, the commission proposed that county or borough rates be levied, to be paid on the basis of the success of the children in examinations in reading, writing and arithmetic. Such levies were not introduced, but the Revised Code of 1862 brought 'payment by results' to the schools. One of the effects was to discourage any attention to subjects and activities other than those examined for purposes of grant. There was thus no official support for the inclusion of physical education in the scheme of instrumentary education planned for working-class children.

The militarists, influenced by the Crimean War and the French crisis, however, advocated drill and physical exercises in the schools as part of national preparedness. In 1862 Lord Elcho moved in the House of Commons that 'for the increase of bodily as well as mental aptitudes of children for civil, industrial as well as for possible Military Service . . . encouragement and aid should be given for the extension of the practice of systematised gymnastic training'. This the government rejected on the grounds of additional cost, for the 3s 8d per child involved an increase of 25 per cent on the maximum grant.[31]

Other propagandists with wider views of the benefits of physical education were active too. Herbert Spencer devoted one of four essays on education published between 1854 and 1859 to physical education. He attacked unscientific attitudes to the physical welfare and upbringing of children, in particular the 'utter disregard'

83

of such matters in girls' schools. He advocated a 'physical morality' so that breaches of the laws of health would be regarded as 'physical sins'. Edwin Chadwick urged a broader view of education for the elementary schools. In 1868 he told a crowded meeting of the Association for the Promotion of Social Science that 'the elementary school should be a place of physical and mental activity', whereas he found the length of time spent at school was shown by the lethargy and dull facial expression of the children. As the result of the application of the Revised Code of 1862 infant schools as such had almost disappeared. He urged the inclusion of physical activities and the introduction of medical inspection for schoolchildren.[32] John Ruskin also advocated that physical education should be given an important place. He thought schools should be built in open country where 'riding, running, all the honest personal exercises of offence and defence and music should be the primal heads of this bodily education'.[33] The most indefatigable supporter of physical education, however, was Dr Mathias Roth, who had studied Ling's system. He urged the introduction of the Swedish system, rejecting Archibald MacLaren's method, and waging a personal campaign to achieve his aim.[34]

By 1870 all that remained in the elementary school for the children of the poor was a certain amount of drill, chiefly for practical disciplinary purposes, and gymnastic exercises in a very few schools. The Revised Code had discouraged physical work, the infant schools in particular suffering from the constriction of their curricula. Gymnastics and drill were spreading in the private schools and the public schools, to play a minor role alongside the established and exalted team games. The work of the propagandists for physical education eventually bore fruit, for the Act of 1870 brought a permissive clause allowing drill to count for attendance, and hence for grant, in the elementary schools (see next chapter), while eight years later Dr Roth's constant advocacy resulted in the introduction of Ling's system of gymnastics by the London School Board.

The isolated and sporadic developments in England before 1870 contrast markedly with the early establishment of systems of physical education in continental schools. In Germany, where the early work of Basedow and GutsMuths has been noted already (page 78), the work of J. F. C. L. Jahn associated gymnastics (*Turnen*) with emerging nationalism and liberalism, which meant that gymnastics flourished under tolerant regimes and was suppressed in times of reaction. In the schools Prussia led the way, the original impetus medically inspired. In 1836 Dr Karl Lorinser published a pamphlet in which he criticised the school system for over-emphasis upon book work to the detriment of emotional balance and physical fitness. In the following year the state issued a permissive decree allowing physical exercises in the higher schools, and later measures (1842) prescribed the establishment of gymnasiums and voluntary physical-education classes in boys' secondary schools and training colleges, while in 1862 the subject was made compulsory for boys in the elementary schools. The content and organisation of the work was based upon the ideas of Adolph Spiess, who rejected Jahn's association of gymnastics with political idealism, but sought rather an educational role, stressing systematic physical development and the disciplinary results, a formula much more attractive to the state authorities. Hugh Rothstein introduced Ling's Swedish gymnastics to the Prussian army in 1860, and some aspects of this system eventually merged into the work in Prussian schools.[35]

Similarly the work of P. H. Ling in Sweden and Franz Nachtegall in Denmark was linked with strong nationalist feeling. Ling developed the work of Pestalozzi and GutsMuths; his own original contribution was based upon his study of anatomy and physiology and his empirical studies. He placed a high value upon 'free-standing' exercises and upon the correction of postural defects. In Sweden, physical education was made compulsory in the secondary schools in 1820 and in the elementary schools in

1824. Ling's work was developed for schoolchildren by his son Hjalmar, who systematised exercises, devising the lesson based upon the 'table' of movements classified according to their anatomical effect. Great care was taken to select exercises appropriate for children of different ages and to ensure progressive development. Nachtegall's fame does not rest upon original contributions to the subject matter but upon his work as a teacher and organiser of physical education. In Denmark, official encouragement of gymnastics in secondary schools dates from 1809, and it was made compulsory in elementary schools in 1814. Further measures came in the following decade: a *Manual of Gymnastics* for elementary schools in 1828 and in the same year a Teachers' Course in gymnastics. However, the link with military gymnastics imposed the dead hand of the militarists, effectively preventing the development of work with teachers and limiting the value of what was done in schools.

Developments in the United States are more nearly parallel to those in Britain. The general impression is of individual initiative and not of widespread uniform innovation. The militarists had little success in achieving systematic military drill in the public schools (in the American sense of 'public', ie state) and the colleges, until the Civil War, when many schools adopted such work, the Morrill Act of 1862 making military drill compulsory in state colleges. The military influence, however, faded quickly after 1865, concern for the national interest being reflected in the sponsorship of activities leading to sound health rather than in work of direct military relevance. German gymnastics were introduced to Boston as early as the 1820s but enthusiasm quickly waned. Later *Turnen* grew in importance, but tended to flourish only amongst expatriates, the real spreading of this system of gymnastics coming after the Civil War. Fellenberg's ideas were introduced in a number of colleges and academies in the 1820s and the following decade, but attention seems to have been focused on manual training rather than gymnastics—an understandable priority in view of the proximity of undeveloped land.

The outstanding individuals who worked first of all privately but who later influenced a number of school boards were Catherine Beecher and Dio Lewis. The latter established in 1861, at Boston, an institute for training teachers, which lasted for some years. The outstanding single development, however, was at Amherst College, where Dr Edward Hitchcock started a programme of physical education in 1861 and was appointed Professor of Hygiene and Physical Education, a professional status not acquired elsewhere in the United States for many years and one not yet achieved in England![36]

Again parallel to developments in England, there was a growing popular interest in sport in the United States in the 1830s and 1840s, with evidence of a similar high value put upon physical activities in their relationship to the moral and spiritual aspects of man's life. The development of sport accelerated in the 1850s, with baseball and rowing to the fore; inter-college fixtures were established, and the Caledonian Games began to be prominent events, presaging the development of track and field athletics.[37]

5

Militarism versus social reform
1870–1902

In the schools there were children in every stage of illness. Children with adenoids, children with curvature, children in every stage of neglect and dirt and suffering . . . It is quite clear I was elected to fight the battle of the slum child.

Margaret McMillan, quoted in
G. A. N. Lowndes, *Margaret McMillan*, 52

While the children of the rich play too much, the children of the poor do not play at all. They do not know how to play; they have no place to play if they did.

Sir John Gorst, *The Children of the Nation*, 212

In considering the development of physical education in the elementary schools during this period, it is clear that the content of the work was restricted severely by physical constraints. Very large numbers of children had to occupy very small working spaces. Therefore some form of drill seemed imperative. Such concentration on drill would obviously be approved by the militarists, and by others who believed that physical training should complement an instrumentary education. They saw the result, the acquisition of the physical equivalent of literacy, as paying dividends in better and more obedient workers, servants and soldiers. Evidence of the physical deterioration of the population as the result of conditions in the industrial towns was accumulating and the accessibility of schoolchildren made them the focus of concern for personal health in the interests of national efficiency. As Dr Mackenzie wrote:

> ... the school child has for a generation been under the direct control of the State in one of his many relations. And the school child, easily seen, easily examined, easily described, has enabled us to crystallise the conception of personal hygiene and add to that the possibilities of remedial measures.[1]

Such interest in schoolchildren would seem inevitably to lead to concern over medical care and supplementary feeding. However, there was bitter opposition to any attempt to increase public responsibility for any aspect other than the rudimentary education of the children of the poor. Economic and moral arguments were used against the assumption by the state of responsibility for physical care. The prevailing attitude was that the sick and hungry ought to be aided by voluntary charitable agencies and by the Poor Law authorities. Dire moral results were forecast if measures of reform, such as the proposal put to the London School Board that meals be provided chargeable to the rates were introduced. *The Times* condemned this idea as 'a policy which . . . will inevitably tempt a large class of parents to starve or half-starve their boys and girls in order to escape a burden to which they are legally subject and which they are very well able to bear'.[2]

Sir John Gorst saw opposition to the 'pauperising' of the poor by measures of relief as consistent with the view that 'It is better to leave the children to perish rather than interfere with the moral dignity and independence of the parent.'[3] This viewpoint had to be challenged by teachers, medical officers and social reformers with first-hand experience of the schools. To them it was evident that the schools could not successfully educate children who were filthy, verminous, diseased and famished. It was the task of the reformers to show, in Beatrice Webb's words, 'the irrelevance of charity' and to win the acceptance of national responsibility for these and other distressing social conditions. Government action was not initiated until 1906 and 1907, and by then motives, other than the purely altruistic, had been provided by the shocked response to the staggeringly large proportion of unfit recruits to the forces during the South African War. Sir Frederick Maurice pointed out that of every five men wishing to enlist in the army only two had the physical capacity to serve more than two years. Even so, to overcome resistance to progress the influence of powerful individuals was needed.

MILITARISM REFLECTED IN DRILL

The militarists argued that as the upper and middle classes financed the elementary schools by paying rates and taxes, it was a modest requirement that some return should be made to the state in the form of the initial drilling of the children as a preparation for their later military training. Such military drill and training should be developed in the post-school years in continuation classes and the Volunteer Corps. It was considered that desirable disciplinary results would be evident too. A basic belief in the effectiveness of transfer of training encouraged the view that the way to civilise the 'street arabs' and 'hooligans' was to drill them into habits of instant obedience, a training held to be eminently suitable for the development of the 'character' of the recipients.

The Education Act of 1870 was necessitated by the failure of the voluntary societies to effect an adequate national system of elementary education, in spite of their enormous achievements in the dissemination of literacy. The foundation of the school boards was followed by a massive increase in the number of school places.[4] The Act made no provision for physical education but the New Code of Regulations for grant, enforced in 1871, allowed attendance of boys at drill, under a competent instructor, of not more than forty hours a year to be counted as school attendance. Instruction was to be given by drill sergeants, and their drill based on the *Field Exercise Book*.

The legislation was merely permissive and the consequent slow growth in the number of schools where boys were drilled indicates apathy, if not overt resistance, to this form of physical activity.[5] What was attempted ranged from military manoeuvres, which the boys liked, to squad drill made unutterably boring by unimaginative and unintelligent instructors obsessed with a passion for repetition and finicky detail. Enthusiasts were found in remote country schools as well as in the large towns and cities. At the GWR school at Swindon, the boys formed squares, prepared to receive cavalry and skirmished in open order in the streets, to their evident enjoyment.[6] Though intended for boys, drill was soon being encouraged as an activity for girls. At some centres units of Volunteer Cadets were established. For example at Manchester, Charles Hughes reported the high standard of drill of both boys and girls, and the contribution of the teachers to the work of the cadet force, which had enlisted 300 boys. Significantly Hughes quoted as an argument in favour of this development, 'In large towns, the boys will be glad to come to the school board playgrounds for drill, for they long for exercise and cannot easily get cricket.'[7] Lord Wolseley regretted that a military organisation with drill was not attached to every school board, while the Earl of Meath's Lads' Drill Association advocated universal physical training for boys up to the age of eighteen.[8]

Drill remained an integral part of the systems of physical training developed by the superintendents of physical exercise appointed by the large school boards. The first instructors appointed had been concerned entirely with drilling children as they would squads of recruits, but later developments included schemes based upon lists of exercises thought suitable for the children. Thomas Chesterton, Superintendent of Physical Exercises for the London School Board, a former chief instructor in the Army Gymnastics Staff at Aldershot, claimed that his 'system', developed in army schools, was compounded from the best existing exercises and was approved by a number of doctors. His ambition was to teach children 'as much drill as a recruit has before he begins rifle drill'. From 1889 onwards the Board held an annual competition for a banner awarded by the Royal Society of Arts. Later, physical exercises were included, but there was no lasting interest and from 1896 annual displays replaced the competitions.[9] The school boards at London and Birmingham supplied staves, dumb-bells, and horizontal and parallel bars to their schools, while other cities adopted similar schemes combining drill and physical exercises.[10] The militarists' claim that drill and physical training improved discipline achieved official recognition and support. The Code of 1890 recognised attendance at 'suitable physical exercises' as eligible for grant on the same basis as drill, while the Code of 1894 went further, stating that the higher rate of grant for Discipline and Organisation would not be paid unless provision were made for 'Swedish or other drill, or suitable exercises'.[11] Grants under this heading were allowed at 1s or 1s 6d per pupil according to the Inspector's report.

The disciplinary value of drill was everywhere recognised, for it seemed the only way of assembling large numbers of children in restricted spaces, and of moving them safely from one part of a school to another. Spencer describes the method of ensuring an orderly end to the 'rough and tough' playtime in his school at Swindon, when sharp retribution was meted out for any breach of the rigid rules for organising the boys and getting them back into school. In the early years of the schools, particularly when compulsory attendance was enforced by the prosecution of recalcitrant parents, the free use of corporal punishment and a rigid code of external discipline seemed the only possible means of quelling ill-disciplined and even riotous children. Spencer describes fighting between boys from different parts of the town, and the schoolmaster's quelling of a riot by caning the ringleader in front of the school. It is against this background that his evaluation of the disciplinary effects of drill must be viewed:

It was all crude and unsuitable, calculated no doubt to arouse a military spirit, which except for externals it did not. But it was good for us; of that I am sure. My father, a John Bright Liberal didn't object. Everybody outside Bedlam is against war and its foolishness and waste. But as a teaching in smartness, in instant obedience, which some situations in life demand, it was justified. Our boys would have behaved well in a shipwreck.[12]

A disciplined and orderly response was obviously necessary for such tasks as ensuring the swift evacuation of such large schools as the London three-deckers. Miss Kingston reported with pride that some 1,500 children could be cleared from the premises in two or three minutes. Others made wider claims for drill, Colonel Fox seeing its influence carried over into good citizenship while the Earl of Meath regarded it as a means of combating rowdyism and riotous behaviour in the streets.

The scheme of drill and physical exercises may be evaluated in terms of the claims made for them. Clearly the application of recruit drill was of little avail as military training. If it had an initial appeal it was because all boys at some time enjoy playing soldiers, though it tends to be an ephemeral interest. It obviously had some attraction for youths with no other suitable outlets for expending their physical energies. When such drill was repetitive, boring and tedious, particularly when applied to physically weak and puny children, undoubtedly the result was a marked disenchantment with the entire proceedings. Far from developing military enthusiasm it must have done much to quell it. The systems were also of little value in ensuring the systematic physical development of the children. It is easy to gain a false idea of what was achieved from descriptions of the annual exhibitions and from the evaluation of the Superintendents of Physical Exercises of their own work. H. B. Philpott's picture of the work in London schools differs vastly from Chesterton's accounts of the application of his 'system':

> It is to be feared that many teachers carry out this part of their duties in a rather unsympathetic spirit. Some, especially teachers of the old school, begrudge the time taken from ordinary studies; others feel the hopelessness of accomplishing anything useful in the way of physical development in the very short time at their disposal: others again are obsessed by the display idea and waste time on trivial matter . . . which would be much better spent in getting a little vigorous work out of the children.[13]

The only schools really efficient in physical training were the

93

resident schools and the Day Industrial Schools (reformatory schools) where the boys had nearly a full hour's hard physical exercise every day. This contrasted markedly with the sparse allocation of time in ordinary board schools. The feeding and health of the children in these 'special' schools were also cared for, so that they were able to benefit from the systematic exercise, unlike so many in the board schools. The schemes of physical exercises combined with drill generally had very limited effect on the physical development of elementary-school children.

On the other hand, the value of a drilled response in aiding the discipline and organisation of schools which were grossly overcrowded and lacking space for games is evident, especially for those children in the first generation in the schools who attended against their own (and their parents') wishes and whose co-operation had to be enforced. In the long run, however, there were stronger agencies than drill for ensuring better discipline. Chief among these was the growth of a humanising spirit amongst teachers, which Philpott saw as

> ... the chief means of making the schools the great social force they have undoubtedly become. There are districts in London, once the despair of social reformers and religious workers, where the planting of a Board School seems almost to have regenerated the neighbourhood, diminishing lawlessness, improving the manners and appearance of the children, changing the attitude of the parents towards education from one of hostility to one of friendliness and bringing order and decency into some of the most degraded homes.[14]

Charles Booth also noted the beneficial effect of the schools in promoting habits of cleanliness and order, in higher standards of dress and decency, for such beneficial influences were carried from the schools to the homes. A change in attitude too became evident:

> ... when children who have themselves been to school become parents, they are ready to accept and uphold the system, and support the authority of the teachers, instead of being prone to espouse with hand and tongue the cause of the refractory child.[15]

Physical activities do play a major role in the humanising work of teachers which enables them to exert a real influence upon the children and their homes, but these are the games and sports voluntarily developed by the teachers in their own time. In this, drill and physical exercises have no part.

The London School Board showed an early interest in physical training and was the first body effectively to introduce the Swedish system by its appointment of Miss Löfving in 1878.[16] The work was developed vigorously by Miss Bergman, who was employed from 1882 to 1888. By that year 1,312 women teachers had been trained in Swedish methods, which were by then taught in every one of the Board's girls' schools and departments.[17] A most important aspect of Miss Bergman's contribution was that she laid the foundations for the later acceptance of systematic physical education, her displays gaining for Swedish gymnastics powerful supporters among people of influence in government circles. Her scheme of work, physiologically sound, was obviously vastly superior to the work being done with boys, and as it had the advantage of not requiring apparatus it was cheap. She gave evidence to the Cross Commission, influencing its view, so that it reported '. . . against . . . elaborate apparatus for gymnastics . . . looking to the training colleges for a "safe and scientific system of physical training" '.[18] Her work was continued by Miss Strachan and Miss Ely, both of whom she trained. To introduce the Swedish system to boys, Captain Haasum was appointed for six months in 1884, and in 1888 Dr Allan Broman was appointed Organising Master of Physical Exercises. He had, however, to compete against Chesterton, who claimed the Swedish system was unsuitable for boys, and whose courses for teachers proved to be more popular than Broman's. The latter's contract was terminated in 1893, the basic reason being the opposition of the militarists to his work. The girls' schools too were influenced by the diversity of methods. In 1900 Miss Kingston, the Organising Teacher of girls' work, described the use of wands and dumb-bells, anathema to supporters of 'pure' Swedish work.

Running
printed. vo
was

SOCIAL REFORMERS' CONCERN

The social reformers, wishing to relieve the suffering of the children from malnutrition, dirt and disease, made the main planks
in their platform state responsibility for the provision of school
meals, medical inspection and treatment. From the early years of
this period various voluntary agencies worked for the relief of
child neglect. The school built at Rousdon in Devon in 1876
included a kitchen providing penny dinners, such a rare exception
that it won national acclaim.[19] In the following decade there were
many agencies providing clothing, boots and shoes, and free or
cheap meals for the most destitute children. Among the best
known of these voluntary associations were the Manchester
Ladies' Health Society and the Visiting Committees of the London
School Board. Investigating committees established by the latter
authority illuminated the size of the problem and the extent of
the relief required. The first enquiry in 1889 revealed that nearly
44,000 out of 341,000 in the Board's schools (or 12.8 per cent)
were habitually in want of food. To these could be added 11,000
children in the same condition in the voluntary schools.[20] Charles
Booth completes the picture:

> Puny, pale-faced, scantily clad and badly shod, these small and
> feeble folk may be found sitting limp and chill on the school
> benches in all the poorer parts of London. They swell the bills of
> mortality as want and sickness thin them off, or survive to be the
> needy and enfeebled adults whose burden of helplessness the next
> generation will have to bear.[21]

The London School Dinners Association was formed, utilising
145 feeding centres. Similar measures were introduced in Birmingham, Glasgow, Edinburgh and Manchester. Again in 1894 and
1898 committees of the London School Board concluded that
voluntary effort alone was not sufficient to meet the needs of
feeding hungry children, but their main recommendation, that
financial aid should be given from the rates, was not accepted.[22]
Any innovation of this sort was held to be highly dangerous,

leading inevitably to the increased degradation and demoralisation of the parents of these neglected children.

Chief among those who aroused the public conscience concerning the physical misery of the children was Margaret McMillan, by her work in Bradford.[23] An eloquent orator and powerful propagandist, she attracted national attention, but had to fight a bitter and prolonged battle against entrenched interests and apathy.[24] Parents, too, opposed her condemnation of the half-time system, for in the mills and in other occupations 4,000 children were working either a morning 'turn', from 6.0 am to 12.30 pm, or an afternoon 'turn', from 1.45 pm to 5.45 pm, and spending the other half of the day at school. Naturally they were too exhausted to derive any benefit from schoolwork. In 1895 she led a deputation to the Home Secretary and wrote a pamphlet, both actions being influential in raising the age of part-timing from eleven to twelve, full-time work starting at thirteen. Despite bitter opposition she secured the appointment of Dr Kerr as Medical Officer to the Bradford Board in 1894 so that the true state of the children could be revealed.[25] The first examination showed that over a hundred had not taken off their clothes for six, seven or even eight months. At last her propaganda evoked a response; the first school clinic was set up in Bradford Town Hall, school nurses were appointed, their work being supplemented later by specialist eye and dental inspections. Her battle for school baths was won finally by the chairman's casting vote in 1897.

Margaret McMillan's work is important not only for the achievements at Bradford but principally because she exerted a most important influence upon powerful officials, who were in a position to initiate and accelerate progress or to hinder and delay developments on a national scale seemingly indefinitely.[26] Lowndes sees her work as providing 'just that crucial background of fact and experimental proof which fired such men as Sir Robert Morant, Sir George Newman and Mr F. W. Jowett to set the administrative and legislative wheels spinning faster in White-hall and Parliament'.[27] The gaining of such support later proved to be vital in the drawing up and implementation of legislation. An example of official initiative can be seen in Sir George Keke-wich's appointment of Dr Eichholz as a member of the ordinary school inspectorate when he failed to convince the Duke of Devonshire of the desirability of appointing at least one medical inspector to the Board of Education.[28] This had an important return, not only in the doctor's work in schools, but also in the value of the evidence he was to give to the Inter-Departmental Committee on Physical Deterioration. An example of initiative by one of HM Inspectors is provided by the work of A. P. Graves as chairman of the Southwark Educational Council which 'started a crusade for the provision of playing fields in slum areas'.[29]

Margaret McMillan, as a Socialist member of a school board, drew attention to the physical suffering of children, indirectly illustrating that a national system of physical education would be ineffective unless malnutrition and disease were remedied first. Other left-wing writers condemned the philosophy which under-lay the poverty of the provision made for working-class children.[30] J. W. Martin wrote that the teachers of London were bewildered by the variety of systems of physical exercises sponsored over the years, and he condemned the poverty of what was offered. His wish that the best parts of the physical education of the public schools should one day be available to every young Briton seems Utopian in the social context of his time.[31] The National Union of Teachers in its advocacy of one national system of education supported the ideal of vastly improved schooling for working-class children, with the removal of distinctions in the quality and quantity of the provisions made for middle-class and for working-class children. A wider conception of physical education, to include the provision of playing fields, swimming baths and gymnasia for the elementary schools, was implicit in the demands of the reformers who condemned the existing dichotomy.

Certain school boards were concerned to broaden the base of their physical education as far as they could within the framework of the law. The London Board had a liberal and enlightened approach, from its early days wishing to include swimming in its programme. There were two difficulties: firstly that of facilities, for of the twenty-five baths in London only three were prepared to offer special terms for children; secondly and insuperably the legal prohibition, for the Board discovered that it was not empowered to build its own baths or to pay for children to attend the existing baths. A major step forward was contained in the Code of 1890, for it allowed swimming to count for attendance purposes. The London Board built two baths of its own and used the borough councils' baths, so that about 50,000 children received instruction in summer, between 14,000 and 15,000 learning to swim each year. Teachers worked voluntarily to develop swimming as a sport. The London Schools Swimming Association awarded proficiency certificates and organised district championships and a central championship.[32]

The main positive moves to remedy the deficiencies of provision for the children came from teachers who sponsored and developed the growth of popular games for their pupils. Teachers and pupils revelled in the freedom of games compared with the restriction and boredom of drill. From 'side games' in the playground, matches with neighbouring schools developed. The major progress in the organisation of association football in the 1880s was reflected in developments in the schools. Many teachers saw in the game 'a simple, ready and pleasant means of physical education'. School clubs grew to associations: the formation of the South London Schools Football Association in 1885 was the beginning of a national movement which, it was claimed, 'has done more for the real physical well-being of the boys of this country than all the drill and callisthenic exercises yet introduced'.[33] The work of teachers meant much self-sacrifice on their part and there were many handicaps. The chief hindrance was the shortage of playing fields; many schools even lacked playgrounds. The major benefits of games were seen in terms of better relationships between masters and boys (girls too became active participants in the athletic and swimming sports organised by the sports associations), and in better attitudes of pupils to school work. For the first time on a large scale, working-class children were being introduced to pleasurable physical activities and pastimes.

However, the relatively small number of schools gaining the top grant for discipline after 1895 illustrates the restricted development of systems of physical exercise—due to the dearth of facilities and of trained teachers. Within a mile radius of Charing Cross 30,000 children were in schools without a square yard of playground, and similar conditions were common in the built-up centres of other towns and cities.[34] The Enclosure Acts and the rapid filling-in of space resulting from the mushroom growth of the industrial towns meant the loss of open spaces for the urban population generally. The Public Health Act of 1848 allowed money from the rates for the establishment and maintenance of public parks, so that gradually some progress was made, though the centres of most towns became completely built up during a brief period while suburbs grew in the surrounding countryside. To remedy the lack of facilities the London Playing Fields' Committee, a voluntary charitable organisation, was formed in 1890, to be followed by a number of similar bodies in provincial centres. These organisations surveyed existing facilities, raised funds and agitated to influence local authorities to increase and improve playing fields and amenities. The provision of playing fields in the parks was crucial to the development of games in the elementary schools.

The enterprise of the major school boards, such as London and Birmingham, was exceptional. Other areas were slow to trouble with providing physical activities in the elementary schools. The minutes of the Norwich School Board illustrate the problems which had to be faced nationally. The Norwich Board's initial difficulties were to create over 3,000 additional school places and to accommodate the 'gutter' children, 'vicious, half-naked and dirty' who upset discipline in the schools and aroused objections from the parents of other children. The board found they lacked the legal power to provide even the simplest article of clothing, and their plans to include two bathrooms in a new school were refused by the Education Department. A drill instructor was employed from 1876–82 when his services were dispensed with as a measure of economy! The board appointed its first inspector, an enthusiast for drill, in 1888, and he persuaded the members to appoint another instructor and to make drill compulsory, the first mass drill being held in 1892. The first mention of games occurs early in the 1880s, though the development of a football association was delayed for some years. In 1895 some fifty boys from the schools were taught to swim by a swimming club, though the board's request for the development of a swimming bath in the river in 1900 was rejected because the estimated cost was considered too great. Nothing was done for the girls in games or swimming.

For the children attending schools in country districts very little was possible. Many children in cities, towns or country districts had as their only experience of organised physical activity a perfunctory drill—limited by lack of space in many instances to desk drill. For the dirty, diseased and under-nourished children who comprised a considerable proportion of the total number, physical exercise was at best an irrelevance, at worst positively harmful. In the wake of the acceptance of the social reformers' revolutionary notion that the feeding of starving children must be a national responsibility, Swedish drill was eventually sponsored as a national system in the schools. As already seen, in 1902 Sir Frederick Maurice's article *Where to Get Men*, which drew attention to the large proportion of unfit recruits for the services in the South African war, caused widespread repercussions.[35] To ensure the greater physical fitness of schoolchildren as the basis of the health of the populace the Board of Education issued a *Model Course of Physical Training* based upon military drill and a series of exercises, this is discussed in the next chapter. A violent reaction occurred and another battle was joined.

NATIONALISM AND PHYSICAL EDUCATION IN CONTINENTAL
SYSTEMS

Continental systems of physical education during this period show the close bond between nationalist sentiment, the associated notion of military preparedness, and physical education in the schools. This is seen in the Scandinavian systems. In Sweden, the military connection dominated work in schools so that dull, rigid routines became the order of the day. In Denmark, the development of gymnastics in the community was closely associated with rifle clubs. A reaction against such a restricted approach was inspired by developments in the folk high schools and the resulting *Manual of Gymnastic Exercises* of 1899 showed the preference for Swedish gymnastics rather than the Danish-German system previously sponsored in the schools. Another ameliorating factor in Denmark was the introduction and growth of games and sports with an associated playground movement. The development of sports in Sweden, however, was delayed until the turn of the century.[36]

The direction of physical education in the schools towards narrow military ends was particularly marked in Germany. The Central Physical Training Institute was controlled jointly by the Prussian Ministries of Education and War. In 1860 the aim of the work in the schools was stated specifically:

> Gymnastic training . . . is closely associated with the system of military training at present used in the royal army. Care must therefore be taken that, apart from the importance of physical training for education and health, the opportunity is offered directly to prepare the nation for war through the proper practice of gymnastics in the schools.[37]

Under Prussian control after 1870 nationalist sentiment dominated the course of physical education in Germany. Nationalism resulted in a stress upon the value of work to remedy the physical degeneration of youth and, particularly in secondary education, was associated with attacks upon intellectualism. Gymnastics, involving in the primary schools a period of an hour each day and in the secondary schools from two to three hours weekly after 1892, were developed in the schools as an instrument of the national policy to create healthy and obedient servants. The position of gymnastics in the schools was reinforced by the importance of the *Turnvereine*, the gymnastic societies, in German society. This movement was divested of its early liberal and revolutionary associations, so that the *Deutsche Turnerschaft* became ostensibly politically neutral. The *Deutsche Turnerbund*, founded in 1899, was strongly anti-semitic and nationalist in outlook.

The *Turner* movement strongly opposed the growth in the community of sports and recreative activities, because of their foreign origin and because they were not linked to nationalist sentiment. But sport grew fast in the 1880s and 1890s, receiving an increased fillip in the latter decade with the birth of the Olympic movement. These developments were reflected in the secondary schools in the introduction of games and in the development of a strong playground movement which aimed to supplement the work done in gymnastics. The establishment in 1891 of the Central Committee for the Promotion of National and Youth Games in Germany marks the gaining of official approval of games, and henceforward the provision of recreation was also associated with strong nationalist feeling.[38]

Developments in the United States provide some interesting parallels with England. In both countries the educational system was expanding rapidly to cater for ever-increasing numbers of children. After the Civil War there was a swift decline in military drill in American schools and colleges, so that by 1899 it was estimated that drill was included in less than 5 per cent of high schools.[39] Medical influence was exerted on work in the schools in two ways. Firstly, many of the pioneering individuals in physical education were themselves qualified in medicine and therefore stressed the therapeutic function. Men such as Dr Dudley Sargent and Dr William G. Anderson established work with a strong remedial bias, stressing too the value of a scientific approach to the acquisition of fitness and health through physical exercises. Courses for the training of teachers were founded as the result of individual initiative, but the products of these courses had most influence outside the public schools—in the women's colleges, the athletic clubs and the YMCA. Secondly, medical influence upon the schools was inspired by the growing concern for the physical deterioration of the population, which in the United States as in England was the consequence of the growth of cities and the resultant congested way of living. Medical inspection and compulsory physical exercises were introduced and playgrounds provided as remedial measures. Again innovation was slow and sporadic. As early as 1868 the Bureau of Education had advocated the importance of hygiene and health education, and had sought to influence school administrations by describing the type of medical inspection already introduced into schools in certain European countries. However, it was not until 1894 that medical inspection in the United States' schools was introduced on a significant scale, and even in 1905 it was provided in fifty-five cities only.[40]

The awakening of the social conscience in the 1890s was typified by the work of numerous individuals and societies rather than by municipal or state initiative. In the city slums the establishment of a settlement movement, partly inspired by the example of Canon Barnett at Toynbee Hall, in London, increased the demand for educational reform. Workers at these settlements were connected directly with the appointment of the first school doctors in 1897, with the provision of classes for handicapped children, and with the provision of school meals.[41] Similarly, pressure from two groups, the Turners and the Women's Christian Temperance Union, had much to do with the introduction of state laws making physical exercises compulsory in schools. The first state to enact such a law was Ohio in 1892 (although a precedent on a modified scale existed in California from 1866 to 1879), and a number of other states followed soon afterwards.[42] Voluntary agencies, many connected with churches, worked to establish summer camps and playgrounds, the latter especially in the densely populated cities. Individual and group initiative was later reinforced by municipal support, with the result that by 1900 many cities provided playgrounds for use mainly during the summer vacations.

The rise of athletic sports in the community had become an organised movement during these years, associations for baseball, lacrosse and basketball being formed before 1900. The American public schools, however, were affected little by such developments:

> School physical education was largely physical training with its emphasis on health, correction of physical defects such as poor posture, and mental discipline through gymnastics and callisthenics. School administrators allotted fifteen to thirty minutes daily for physical exercises in some schools, while many children had no physical education at all.[43]

Clearly, in American schools as in English schools at this time, a great deal needed to be done, by a vastly greater provision of facilities and by a re-allocation of priorities, before physical education could make its contribution to the total education of the children.

6

Therapeutic physical education 1902–19

What we have been doing from Whitehall for children has infinitely bigger certainties and far more wide-reaching possibilities than any work in England. I believe truly that these next steps as to [medical] treatment, with all the various possibilities they are opening up, are amongst the most crucial things that are being attempted and done in any sphere for the people of this land.

Sir Robert Morant, quoted in
Sir George Newman, *The Building of a
Nation's Health*, 458–9

We have to teach such children how to play: the games of the pavement are better than no games at all; but games of a greater and nobler kind must be taught. The games master, whether paid or unpaid, becomes necessary if the children of the poor are to have the manly and health-giving opportunities of those games which have done so much in forming national character in our public schools.

The Bishop of Ripon in the preface to
R. E. Roper, *Organised Play at Home and Abroad*

Sponsorship of physical education for disciplinary and military reasons, and also the more widely based support for the development of games, remained of considerable importance during the first twenty years of the twentieth century. But the major developments in the assumption by the state of certain responsibilities for the welfare of citizens brought radical changes to the schools; these combined with the acceptance of new standards in educational thought and practice to create a new conception of the subject of physical education. The attempt to link 'physical effects' and 'educational effects' led significantly to the substitution of the title 'physical education' for 'physical training' at times. The most important single measure was the creation of the School Medical Service in 1907, which may be evaluated in the context of the general development of public-health legislation and as part of the creation of the welfare state. In the schools the aim was to eliminate malnutrition, disease, dirt and physical defects by medical care and by the vigorous sponsorship of therapeutic physical training. The educational limitations of this approach were soon evident, as was the contrast between the delight most children took in games and their bored participation in the official tables of exercises. The adoption of a more liberal approach, allowing teacher choice of activity, and the abandonment of the rigid standards inherited from the drill sergeant were developments in physical education parallel to the evolution in content, teaching methods and attitudes of teachers in other subjects of the curriculum.

Sir Frederick Maurice's expression of concern at the small proportion of recruits who were fit for service in the Boer War was the immediate cause of the setting up of the Inter-Departmental Committee on Physical Deterioration. Maurice not only described the physical defects of recruits, but also pointed out that lack of nutrition in youth due to unwholesome feeling and physical neglect could not be remedied later. He called attention, too, to investigation into poverty by Charles Booth and Seebohm Rowntree, supporting the former's plea for a national inquiry. He stressed the importance to the nation of the health of the women and children in the urban communities.[1]

Upper- and middle-class opinion was entrenched in the belief that to extend state responsibility to the physical care of working-class children would be disastrous; the remedy for their physical deficiencies was seen rather to be an intensification of the drilling and exercising of the children in the schools. The Board of Education's *Model Course of Physical Training* (1902) was based entirely upon the drill and exercises of recruits. Part 1 was composed of squad drill, while the prefatory comment to Part 2 (exercises) was 'hats, coats and mufflers interfere much with the freedom of the movements and should be dispensed with as a rule'. The exercises were divided into Deep Breathing, Leg, Marching, Rapid Marching, Gymnastic March (a type of goose-step), Double March, and Hopping and Jumping. Also included were what were termed 'Free Gymnastics', but the restricted use of the adjective is apparent from the instruction, 'All movements in free gymnastics must be performed by word of command. The squad will be formed in two ranks and numbered from right to left.' The exercises included knee bending and stretching (four times per minute!), arm bending and stretching (from the front support position), arm swinging, exercises with staves (for which bar-bells or light dummy rifles might be used), and a miscellaneous assortment of chest-expanding movements, lunging and dumb-bell work. No attempt was made to adapt the exercises to suit children. Many of the movements were anatomically and physiologically unsound; the adoption of rigid positions, with the additional constriction from stiff and jerked movements, were actually harmful for growing children.

'Practical Suggestions' were added for the implementation of this *Model Course*: class teachers were to take the physical training of the children, and NCOs were to train the teachers. Incentives for teachers were provided in the form of Certificates of Competency from the Lads' Drill Association. Cheapness was an obvious merit of the training scheme envisaged. The author of the *Model Course* considered that the social reformers had grossly exaggerated the physical defects of the children in the schools. He estimated that only one per cent were 'weakly and delicate' and claimed that 'for mainly weakly children regular physical training is highly desirable'. The *Model Course* was to be considered as a 'minimum', and to be supplemented by further and more varied physical training or by additional work, including skirmishing, based upon *Infantry Training* (1902) published by the War Office.[2] Circular 452 urged the inspectors to assess the work by its effect upon the 'general bearing and physique of the children'.

The *Model Course* was condemned vehemently by progressives, in particular by the National Union of Teachers and by the advocates of Ling's gymnastics. The writer of an article entitled 'Ramrod and Pipe-clay Over again, or the Stupidity of the "Model" P.T. Course' declared it was monstrous to thrust an unsuitable drill system on to the teachers, and he deplored the Board of Education's sponsorship of schemes already found to be useless by the school boards. He saw the political pressure exerted by the patrons of the Lads' Drill Association as responsible for this retrograde step. He stated bluntly that 'not one in fifty' of the NCO drill instructors was 'capable of teaching the method under discussion intelligently to teachers or scholars'.[3] Despite objections, courses for schoolmasters and schoolmistresses were organised in many areas, certain authorities making attendance at drill compulsory. The spectacle of teachers such as the headmaster of Hethersett British School in Norfolk, then in his thirty-fifth year of service, being drilled with his two daughters, who were his assistants, must have been ludicrous and pathetic. In 1903 the President of the Board of Education received a deputation from the NUT to hear their objections to the *Model Course* and to compulsory drill for teachers. Supporters of Swedish gymnastics, particularly the incensed women of the physical education colleges, added their protest, with the result that an Inter-Departmental Committee was set up 'to render a Model Course, or Courses, adaptable for the different ages and sexes of the children in public elementary schools'.[4] This committee was able to make use of the very comprehensive enquiry of the Royal Commission set up in 1902 as the result of concern for the health of the population.

REPORT OF THE ROYAL COMMISSION ON PHYSICAL TRAINING (SCOTLAND), 1902

This Royal Commission of 1902 had a profound influence, first because it did not limit itself to Scotland but called an impressive number of English witnesses and visited certain schools in England, and secondly because of its very broad interpretation of its terms of reference, particularly of the phrase 'to suggest means by which such [physical] training may be made to conduce to the welfare of the pupils'. The Royal Commission revealed that the existing teaching of physical training was 'inadequate in quantity and quality', for it was rarely allocated more than half an hour a week and was completely unsystematic because teachers were not trained. It showed practical common sense in revealing that lack of facilities in the schools and training colleges were inhibiting progress, and also in evaluating drill for its disciplinary effects. But in recommending that ex-pupils and local clubs be utilised to develop games in the elementary schools it was being unrealistic. It showed wisdom in calling for 'a new conception of education' so that teachers could be weaned from mechanical methods derived from a rigid adherence to the Code, and in refusing to arbitrate between the many 'systems' of physical training, the claims for which were submitted in detail by their respective advocates. It was convinced of the necessity of a national system, but declared roundly that military drill was unsuitable for small children.

The committee examining the *Model Course* of 1902 took its cue from the Royal Commission and rejected the scheme because it was not based upon 'physical exercise as a necessary element in a well-ordered course of general education for children'. Instead it drew up a syllabus of work suitable for children, encouraging teachers to choose from the material presented. It also mentioned vaguely the need for indoor working space and echoed the unrealistic hopes for voluntary aid in games, at the same time revealing the existing paucity of facilities. The syllabus included appropriate advice to teachers on the selection of exercises and the construction of progressive programmes of work.[5] The rule for the inclusion of children was reversed, a medical examination being recommended for all doubtful cases. The syllabus was in effect a compromise, for the military organisation of the class was retained, but the exercises were based on the Swedish classification.

The grading and selection of the latter were far more systematic and scientific than anything produced previously. The groups of exercises were categorised according to the part of the body they were intended to benefit: (1) Play, Running or Marching; (2) Preliminary Positions and Movements; (3) Arm Flexions and Extensions; (4) Balance Exercises; (5) Shoulder Exercises and Lunges; (6) Trunk Forward and Backward Bending; (7) Trunk Turning and Sideways Bending; (8) Marching; (9) Jumping; (10) Breathing Exercises. This syllabus was the official basis of work in the schools from 1904 to 1909. A weakness was that it was interpreted in many areas by army-trained 'specialists' introduced with the *Model Course*. Indeed the Board of Education itself had appointed Colonel G. M. Fox, a former inspector of army gymnasia, as Inspector of Physical Training in Schools, a post he retained until 1908.

One aspect of the Royal Commission's wide interpretation of its terms of reference was the arrangement of the medical examination of 1,200 children in Edinburgh and Aberdeen by Professor Matthew Hay and Dr W. L. Mackenzie in order to ascertain 'the exact physical condition of the children'. The result was to prove the connection between inferior housing and child ill health and malnutrition. Over 19 per cent of the children in Edinburgh were in poor health and nearly 30 per cent were found to be undernourished; the full significance of the enquiry was rammed home:

If the ratios observed by the Examiners be admitted . . . there are in Edinburgh Board Schools 700 cases of unrecognised phthisis (pulmonary consumption) and 458 in Aberdeen, and 1,300 cases of unrecognised heart disease of a dangerous nature in Edinburgh and 250 in Aberdeen. Of lesser ailments there are in the Edinburgh schools 15,000 children affected with disease of the throat and 7,580 in Aberdeen, and 12,000 cases of ear disease in Edinburgh and 2,250 in Aberdeen.

The total school populations were 30,000 and 25,000 respectively. The dangers inherent in any scheme of physical training in those conditions were apparent, as was the imperative need to introduce a scheme of medical inspection to the schools. Next in importance was the feeding of children at school, though the dangers of 'impaired parental responsibility' again loomed large and there was no wish to make school meals a charge on the rates. While the members of the commission accepted their medical officers' opinion of the necessity of medical inspection, they found Dr Mackenzie's view of the function of physical training which today seems most enlightened, particularly unacceptable.[6] To him the fundamental problem was to secure for children 'the nurture necessary to make physical training in school profitable'. Unlike so many other witnesses he viewed drill as being of value solely for disciplinary purposes, regarding spontaneous games and activities as the best means of ensuring physical development. He expressed his doubts of the moral value of drill in outspoken fashion, failing to see why 'the uncriticised ideals of the drill sergeant and the acrobat should be made the model for the free evolution of school life'. For boys in post-school years he could see no value in drill or formal physical training, for he considered that after a ten-hour working day they deserved recreative pursuits. The lengthy cross-examination he was subjected to reveals the antagonism of certain commissioners to his views.

The commissioners showed great interest in the uses made by other nations of their 'sources of national strength'. A. Alexander, formerly Director of Liverpool Gymnasium, and founder of a college and gymnasium at Southport, described developments in physical education in Sweden, Germany, France and the United States. By expressing his view of the unsuitability of military exercises for children, Alexander directed the commissioners from the arguments of the many witnesses who extolled the advantages of military drill for schoolchildren and for post-school adolescents.

The work of the Royal Commission influenced the Inter-Departmental Committee on Physical Deterioration which reported in 1904, supporting the introduction of medical inspection for schoolchildren. This committee's motives are apparent in their statement: 'In a country without military service the period of school life offers the State its only opportunity for taking stock of the whole population and securing to its profit the conditions most suitable to healthy development.' This national duty was not, however, to extend to the provision of food, for despite the advocacy of such diverse witnesses as Sir John Gorst and Dr Macnamara, despite Dr Eichholz's evidence that in London alone, 122,000 children or 16 per cent of the school population were in need of feeding, and despite firm evidence of the inadequacy of the voluntary agencies, the committee saw its paramount duty to be the protection of the community from 'the consequences of the somewhat dangerous doctrine that free meals are the necessary concomitant of free education'. Even so, Professor Mackintosh considered the committee's views represented 'enlightened "administrative" thought' and as such to be in advance of current upper- and middle-class opinion. It is evident that in recommending physical training the committee's main concern was to recruit for the army by using municipal funds to maintain classes for youths after their school days were over, with drill and physical exercises as prominent features. Its restricted view of the provision desirable for working-class boys is revealed by such statements as, 'The older lads could actually be familiarised with the use of the rifle an exercise of no inconsiderable value from the point of view of general education.'

The resistance of the Local Government Board to suggested change is seen in the circulars issued in 1905 which clarified to Boards of Guardians their duties in cases where parental neglect resulted in starving children attending school. In the same year the report of an Inter-Departmental Committee on the Medical Inspection and Feeding of Children confined itself almost exclusively to the 'better organisation of voluntary effort'. Though it warned that in the initiation of medical inspection in schools care must be taken to avoid infringing the prerogatives of general practitioners, it also revealed that the local authorities were creating for the first time the kind of organisation capable of implementing a national policy.

During these years when officials were contemplating change with misgivings, or expressing resistance to innovation, political pressures for state assumption of responsibility for the physical welfare of children reached a climax. Left-wing political organisations had called for action for many years. The main planks in the socialist educational platform were free education and secular education, while trade unionists campaigned for improved educational provision for working-class children. At its inception in 1884 the Social Democratic Federation included in its programme a demand for 'the provision of at least one wholesome meal a day in each school'. Throughout the years socialist and trade-union pressure persisted and grew, though the only relief of distress amongst the children was achieved by voluntary agencies.[7] The opportunity for legislation came with the Liberal landslide of 1906, which brought a substantial number of Labour members to the House of Commons too. The new government brought in a vigorous programme of social reform, including legislation regulating hours of work, minimum wages, housing and town planning, and establishing old-age pensions and labour exchanges. Included, too, were the Education (Provision of Meals) Act, a permissive measure allowing local authorities to spend up to a halfpenny rate on the actual cost of food, and the Education (Administrative Provision) Act of 1907 which set up the Medical Department of the Board of Education and provided for the medical inspection of schoolchildren. The upper and middle classes doubted the wisdom of such action, Professor Mackintosh reveals the prevalent state of mind; 'It was', he says, 'a leap in the dark to make deductions about the communal responsibility for persons—even children and their nutrition.'[8] However, he discerns parallel forces for change in the transformation of the Poor Law Infirmaries into general hospitals, and in the medical opinion that medical expenses for a poor woman in childbirth should be met by the rates. Concern about tuberculosis, too, was important; indeed this he sees as 'the spearhead of the campaign for a personal health service at the beginning of the century'; this disease was so infectious that it struck without respect of person or class. It may be noted that Sir John Gorst, in presenting his case for the state assumption of the care of children, placed concern for public safety from contagious disease as the first grounds of intervention.[9]

MEDICAL FINDINGS—A PRELUDE TO ACTION

Once legislation was passed it was the duty of the chief officials to implement the new policy effectively, and in this Sir Robert Morant exerted a crucial influence. It is very doubtful whether in 1907 Parliament would have supported the establishment of a complete medical service; indeed the implications were that the legislative measures had very limited aims. Members believed that medical inspection in the schools would reveal defects which should then be treated by family doctors. It was anticipated that inspection would reveal those children suffering from undetected eye-strain or from the effects of physical training, and that perhaps its most valuable function would be to provide an anthropometric survey which would indicate the extent of the physical deterioration of the population. Clearly Morant, who had been impressed by Margaret McMillan's work (see p 97ff), had more ambitious aims. He visualised from the outset the extension of the work of medical officers to treatment, and selected staff whom he knew would push ahead vigorously. He expressed his conviction thus:

> What we have been doing from Whitehall for children has infinitely bigger certainties and far more wide-reaching possibilities than any work in England. I believe truly that these next steps as to [medical] treatment, with all the various possibilities they are opening up, are amongst the most crucial things that are being attempted and done in any sphere for the people of this land.[10]

He chose Dr George Newman to develop energetically the work of the medical branch, while Newman was to be 'encouraged from the centre' by Newsholme, the Chief Medical Officer of the Board of Health.

Newman's legal powers seemed fairly limited, for while the Act of 1907 made it the duty of the 328 local authorities to provide for the medical inspection of children, treatment was left as 'a power which the authority might exercise under certain conditions'. However, he set out to encourage actively the local authorities' adoption of a wide interpretation of their powers. The task of the authorities was '. . . viewed in a broad light as comprehending all influences, whether they be educational, preventive or creative, which ameliorate or improve the physical condition of children during their school life'.[11] Local initiative in the establishment of clinics, in the appointment of school nurses for giving treatment, in the establishment of open-air schools was described and praised, while other authorities were urged to emulate the example shown. Medical inspection revealed that disease, dirt and malnutrition existed in abundance. It became evident too that the basic problems were deep-rooted in society and that remedial measures confined to children in school could achieve only a partial success.

Official statistics reveal the extent of the problems. Of 1,000 children examined in the poorer districts of Bradford in 1906 only 3 per cent were 'clean', 26 per cent were 'somewhat dirty', 61·5 per cent were 'dirty' and 9·5 per cent 'very dirty'. By 1908 the respective figures had improved to 18·5 per cent, 42 per cent, 36 per cent and 3·5 per cent, but whether this was entirely due to the beneficial effect of the cleansing measures taken as claimed by the Chief Medical Officer, or whether the children were being cleaned up for subsequent medical inspections is problematical.[12] Verminous heads and bodies abounded. The first examinations in Ipswich revealed 26 per cent of the girls were infected, while the general low level was revealed by the examination of girls in Standard 7 at Gillingham in Kent, where, despite their lessons in hygiene and though old enough to look after their own cleanliness, 15·7 per cent were verminous, 73·1 per cent did not clean their teeth and 70·9 per cent came to school with dirty hands.[13] It was useless to cleanse the children of vermin in schools if they were reinfected immediately at home, so that the compulsory cleansing of homes had to be undertaken. The difficulty of educating parents conditioned to squalor is also revealed: a doctor in Norwich commented, 'In many cases it is impossible to convince the parent that head lice are not natural inhabitants of the scalp.'[14] It became evident, too, that in some poorer homes the only washing facility was a small bowl, and until cleansing stations were provided many of the older children had no recollection of ever having had a hot bath. The ultimate sanction for cleanliness was legal action; in 1909 in London the parents of 296 children were prosecuted.

Oral hygiene was utterly neglected with the consequent prevalence of decayed teeth. The first dental clinic, privately sponsored, was established in Cambridge in 1907. By 1909 the widespread nature of dental decay was apparent: in Flintshire 68·5 per cent of the boys and 68·8 per cent of the girls in urban areas, and 80·5 per cent of the boys and 65·7 per cent of the girls in rural areas, suffered from four or more decayed teeth. A detailed investigation in Birmingham showed the number of unsaveable teeth increased with age, about one-third of decayed teeth being unsaveable after the age of eight or nine. So urgent was the need for treatment that certain local authorities used their initiative to establish dental clinics. Other widespread conditions needing urgent medical care included contagious skin diseases such as the 'itch' and ringworm, nose and throat infections, eye disease and vision defects, ear disease and defective hearing and tuberculosis.

The resistance encountered by school doctors is illustrated well from Norwich records. Here the education committee was prepared to take action and in its establishment of an open-air school in 1908 and its employment of a school dentist in the following year it was one of the few innovating authorities. The open-air school took only a small proportion of the 122 children (3·3 per cent of the entire school population) suffering from subnormal nutrition. Of 4,032 children examined, 584 (14·4 per cent) required dental treatment because of oral conditions which were affecting their general health, while a further 83·2 per cent needed dental treatment. Spray baths were installed and the doctors campaigned to foster cleanliness, not least by calling for adequate facilities for washing in the schools themselves. Diagnosis of the various ailments was, however, no guarantee of their treatment. The medical staff of the eye infirmary, for instance, supported by the local branch of the British Medical Association believed the local authority ought to provide or pay for treatment of eye defects. The School Medical Officer pointed out his dilemma, in that there was no legal obligation upon the local authority to provide treatment. Moreover there were no Treasury grants available for the purpose, and he believed that once the local authority did accept responsibility for treatment it would make future government aid less likely. In 1911 he found that of the 575 children for whom treatment had been recommended, 29 per cent remained untreated at the end of the year. Contributory causes were parental unwillingness and the disagreement of the family doctor over the necessity of treatment. No real solution was found until 1914 when arrangements for treatment were made with the Jenny Lind Hospital. A constant battle over many years was required to contain and conquer many troublesome conditions. Ringworm is a good example of a highly infectious condition which proved extremely difficult to treat. Segregation, when enforced, required an average absence from school of thirty weeks to effect a cure.

PHYSICAL EDUCATION WITHIN THE SCHOOL MEDICAL SERVICE

The active development of physical education as an integral part of the work of the school medical service was based upon the official *Syllabus* (1909) and the better training of teachers. A new syllabus of hygiene, issued in the same year, stressed the importance of understanding what constituted a healthy school environment, and the Inspectors of Physical Exercises examined the theoretical and practical work of the students in training. An attempt was made to integrate the whole scheme into a national system firmly guided by the Chief Medical Officer. The inspectors were appointed in the medical department, and the local authority medical officers were urged to take an active role in the control of the physical training in their areas. Local authorities were urged to appoint specialist and organising teachers to take classes in physical exercises for teachers and pupil teachers. For the secondary schools a scheme of formal lessons in physical exercises supplemented by games and athletics was visualised.[15] To improve the content of the work a *Revised Syllabus* was issued in 1909. This was 'more definitely Swedish in character' and included a number of recreative items 'to relieve the dullness, tedium and monotony of former lessons'.[16]

The aim of the *Revised Syllabus* was firmly therapeutic. The first chapter broadened the understanding of teachers by dealing with general principles, the physiology of exercise and hygiene. Every effort was made to help teachers interpret the exercises correctly by the inclusion of illustrative sketches and photographs and by the use of simple language. A much simpler form of class organisation was used, though it was still essentially that of the drill squad. Obedience and discipline were basic requirements, but there was also an effort to make the work enjoyable by stressing the value of a cheerful and sympathetic attitude by the teachers, and by introducing dancing-steps and games. A handsome tribute was paid to the moral, social and educational value of games, but the only activities advocated and described were simple running, jumping and ball games, which required as a minimum a couple of soft small balls or bean bags and a little playground space— cheapness was still a valued attribute of a national system. Even these small concessions to the value of enjoyment were resisted and condemned by the devotees of Ling. Margaret Stansfield's view was that 'while we want children to enjoy their lessons, earnest work is in itself a pleasure'.[17] Unwillingness to deviate from the Swedish system was justified by its adherents:

> Teachers of Swedish gymnastics are often accused of fanatical adherence to their own doctrines and an uncompromising hostility to other systems. The divergence between them and the exponents

of most other systems is due to such fundamental differences in principles and aims, that they feel they would be false to their high ideals if they attempted any form of compromise.[18]

To develop the work in schools HM Inspectors accorded physical training special importance. Demonstration lessons were held by specialist inspectors for the benefit of teachers, and the stimulus resulting from the work of organising teachers is also evident from school log books. Also apparent is the constant endeavour of the inspectors to improve physical conditions in the schools, prodding the local authorities and the managers of voluntary schools to enlarge the teaching space, provide cloak-rooms, improve playgrounds and generally enhance the appearance of premises. The educational limitations of the system of physical exercises were not remedied by the *Syllabus* of 1909. *Circular 779* of 1911 and the report of 1912 repeated the board's advice for successful teaching, advocating 'gymnastic games' and dancing to relieve the tedium of work. To encourage the local authorities the Medical Grant Regulations of 1917 stated that the board would in future meet half the cost of all physical training organisers, resulting in forty additional appointments being made during the year.

LACK OF PLAYING FIELDS

When the Code of 1906 allowed organised games to be included in the work of the elementary schools, the benefits foreseen were both physical and moral. The impulse came from an article written by A. P. Graves, HMI, with the support of Lord Londonderry, in *The Contemporary Review* in 1904. He considered that it was of the utmost national importance that the newly founded local education authorities should appropriate enough ground to develop playing fields for both boys and girls. He did not think sufficient initiative had been shown in the schools, quoting as an example worthy of emulation a London school where a combination of physical exercises, games and athletics had achieved most beneficial results. Graves was concerned to show how Sir Robert

Morant's broad conception of physical activities in the primary school could be implemented in practical terms. Morant, in the introduction to the Code of 1904, had stated:

> The School ... must afford them every opportunity for the healthy development of their bodies, not only by training them in appropriate exercises and encouraging them in organised games, but also by instructing them in the working of some of the simpler laws of health. .... The corporate life of the school, especially in the playground, should develop that instinct for fair play and for loyalty to one another which is the germ of a wider sense of honour in later life.

This statement is a marked advance from the concept of an instrumentary education, of the physical equivalent of literacy. It is the application of the ethos of the games-playing public school to the elementary schools, implying a consequent widening of opportunities for working-class children. The bishop of Ripon developed the theme some years later, deploring the inability of town children to play games which he advocated as a means of acquiring health and developing character.

Local authorities made surveys of the facilities in their areas and many introduced schemes based chiefly upon utilising pitches in public parks. The true extent of the shortage of playing fields was revealed by the report of a Departmental Committee in 1912. Public parks and recreation grounds were the main provision. Examples of the scale of facility were included: in Liverpool 7,540, or one-sixteenth of those in average attendance, played games; in Preston the proportion was one-tenth; 3,000 out of 19,000 were catered for in Norwich. As could be foreseen the greatest difficulties were in the congested districts of large towns. The committee proposed to encourage the provision of playing fields in new schools by allowing smaller playgrounds to compensate for the increased cost of buying a field. It also recommended that existing schools be made to conform to certain standards in playing field provision by 1920 and 1925, though this proposal was regarded as a pretext for closing church schools.[19] In any event the arrival of war quashed any proposed legislation. Much was being left to voluntary effort, as R. E. Roper showed in his description of the work of boys brigades, the Boy Scouts, the Happy Evenings Association, the play centres and such provincial establishments as the Birmingham Athletic Institute.[20]

THE EFFECTS OF WORLD WAR I ON THE SCHOOLS

Militarists did not abandon their wish to see physical training in the schools used for the creation of an effectively trained reserve force. The Board of Education had to justify its stress upon therapeutic physical training both before and during the war when pressure was intensified. Newman stated the case against military training in schools in 1910: such a system was unsuitable because it started too late, affected only a portion of the nation (and that the fittest) and excluded girls and women. He stressed the value of preventive work during the 7–14 age period, quoting recent recruiting figures to prove his point. These arguments did not deter Lord Charles Beresford from introducing a bill in 1912 making physical training as pre-military training compulsory up to sixteen years of age, though to allay opposition he included a clause that children were not to be taught the use of weapons.[21] After the outbreak of war the board rejected further calls for military drill and the use of rifles in the schools, as it did Lord Haldane's suggestion for pre-service training, comprising Boy Scout troops in the elementary schools, cadet corps in the second-ary schools and OTC units in the universities to complete a national system.[22] Newman kept to his role, which he conceived as 'promoting the physical efficiency of all children', showing un-exceptionable tact in steering a course between the militarists and the determined opponents of military drill in the schools, who included the trades unions, the NUT and physical educationists.

While the war disrupted many schools, some premises being requisitioned or occupied while others were affected by the loss of teachers to the forces, the initial effects upon the condition of schoolchildren seem to have been beneficial. The board reported:

There is evidence from many quarters that the wave of prosperity caused by good employment, high wages and the allowances made to the families of soldiers and sailors, have a marked effect on the general well-being of school children. In many cases they are better fed and clothed than ever before.

This view was confirmed by a dramatic drop in the number of school meals provided free per week: after a rapid rise to 1,218,238 in October 1914, it declined to under 200,000 in July 1915, and even further, to about 120,000 a year later. The demand for labour affected the schools causing a rapid decrease in the numbers in the senior classes in the elementary schools, and resulting in large numbers of 'early leavers'—boys and girls leaving to take up jobs before completing their courses—in the seondary schools.[23] However, the long-term effects were not beneficial, for by 1916 so many medical and nursing staff had joined the forces that in some areas medical inspection was confined to 'ailing' children. The blockade at sea resulted in food shortages at home, so that in 1916 the board had to prepare schemes of emergency feeding in the schools should the need arise. The remaining winters of the war were periods when the schools were severely affected by sickness, particularly in 1918–19 by the ravages of influenza.

CHILD EXPLOITATION AND NEGLECT OF THE ADOLESCENT

Ten years after the passing of the Acts of 1906 and 1907 the health and well-being of the schoolchild were accepted as being legitimately the concern of the state. The next major step involved the extension of this concern to the adolescent, and the remedy of the evils of half-time attendance at school and the long hours of work engaged in by children of school age. The half-time system, involving up to thirty hours of factory work and attendance at school for thirteen or fourteen hours, obviously made effective education impossible. Wartime conditions, in creating an unsatisfied demand for labour, had extended the system so that in the manufacturing districts children normally left school at thirteen and became half-timers at twelve.[24] R. A. Bray had shown in 1911 the injurious effects of long hours of work upon the education and health of children still at school.[25] These were confirmed by investigations by A. Freeman in Birmingham where a great deal of child labour was employed mainly in shops and street-trading in the poorer central parts of the city; he showed both the physical stress of undue exertion and the consequent demoralisation, for a large proportion of the children were committing offences. Though certain local authorities had bylaws affecting the employment of children in street-trading, more stringent regulations were necessary. An investigation into the physical conditions of outworkers in Norwich in 1912 confirmed that the employed children were more defective physically and worse clad.

In addition, much of the value of the work done by the schools was lost by lack of supervision during the post-school years. Boys were in great demand as a cheap form of labour, especially in large cities, and in the majority of cases employment was chosen simply on the basis of immediate earnings. This could be expected when half the homes, as in Birmingham, were suffering temporarily or permanently from poverty.[26] But after four years (often nomadic) at work suitable only for juveniles, boys of eighteen were fitted only for unskilled labouring, while many had so deteriorated physically that not even this avenue of employment was open to them. Only a third of London's children went into skilled trades or higher education, while half entered 'blind-alley' occupations. A bare minimum of skill was all that was necessary for most jobs in manufacturing industries; employers were indifferent to adolescent needs, and excessive hours of work—the ten-hour day in industry and the seventy-four-hour week in shops—combined with unhealthy conditions of work to restrict physical development. Freeman concluded, 'It is probable that the great majority of the boys of this country are entering manhood physically undeveloped and unfit because of the impossibility of getting physical exercise during this period.'[27] The exploitation of boy labour was not limited to private individuals and firms; the Post Office was also a notorious offender, keeping on only a small fraction of boys as adult workers. Parental influence was minimal and voluntary associations, affecting only some 20–25 per cent of boy workers and that the better portion, could offer little more than tactful guidance. Boys' clubs, which did not affect the lower strata where the greatest need existed, were valued simply for their capacity to provide amusement.

The remedy suggested by both Bray and Freeman was to raise the school-leaving age to fifteen and to continue part-time education to eighteen on the pattern of such firms as Cadbury's at Bourneville in Birmingham. Both stressed the value of a general education and the need for ensuring physical development and fitness. Bray wished the local education authority to retain a power of supervision, to include that of periodic medical inspection. Freeman called for a change of outlook, a sentiment reiterated by the Departmental Committee on Juvenile Employment (the Lewis Committee) in 1917. The committee recommended full-time education to fourteen, with no exemptions, followed by attendance of 8 hours a week or 320 hours a year at continuation classes to the age of eighteen.

THE EDUCATION ACT OF 1918 AND THE SYLLABUS OF 1919

In his statement to the House of Commons in 1918 H. A. L. Fisher gave as his first reason for introducing an Education Bill the need to improve the physical conditions of the young:

> One of the great dates in our social history is the establishment of the school medical service in 1907. We know now, what we should not otherwise have known, how greatly the value of our educational system is impaired by the low physical conditions of a vast number of children, and how imperative is the necessity of raising the general standard of physical health among the children of the poor, if a great part of the money spent on our educational system is not to be wasted. . . .[28]

The bill included the recommendations of the Departmental Committee concerning the extension of the period of schooling, but the inclusion of part-time education to eighteen was postponed for seven years because of the determined opposition of employers. The Education Act of 1918 made it obligatory for local authorities to provide medical treatment and included permissive provisions allowing them to provide holiday or school camps (especially for young persons attending continuation schools), centres and equipment for physical training, playing fields, school baths and swimming baths, and other facilities. The Chief Medical Officer foresaw great opportunities for development:

> The Local Education Authorities throughout England and Wales are now in possession of an adequate and comprehensive instrument for achieving these great national ends. The inestimable good which they have accomplished in ten years, with meagre and somewhat indifferent machinery, affords good promise of their wise and far-seeing use of the new and enlarged opportunity at the door of which they now stand.[29]

Much obviously would depend upon local initiative, but the driving force of the Medical Department remained unimpaired.

Clearly too the syllabus and teaching methods in physical training needed to be reformed to allow greater freedom to the teacher and greater recreative opportunity. Such a change of emphasis also directly reflected those developments in educational and philosophic thought which had been responsible for changes throughout the curriculum since the beginning of the century. Hearnshaw has shown the association between the growth of psychology and that of progressive trends in education, discerning as the most important influence Sir John Adams's *Herbartian Psychology Applied to Education* (1897), which stimulated educational thought by stressing the importance of 'interest' and by questioning the generally accepted notions of formal training. The new ideals of infant teaching, largely continental in origin, partly psychologically inspired, and associated with the names of Froebel and Montessori also exerted a decisive influence by spreading upwards through the curriculum. The main effect of these developments discernible in the schools was towards greater freedom for teacher and pupil.[30] In the light of other curricular changes it was now necessary to reappraise more critically the content and methods of the syllabus, rather than relying on the palliatives such as the introduction of playground games mentioned above. Children had a ready and natural interest in games, so this added another reason for the more active sponsorship of the provision of playing fields and the playing of team games.

The *Syllabus of Physical Training* produced in 1919 stressed a broadened concept of physical education while still retaining its faith in a 'scientific system' of therapeutic exercise. The freedom of the pupil and teacher was emphasised, it being recommended that not less than half the lesson should be devoted to 'active free movements, including games and dancing'. The exercises and 'positions' were by and large those of the 1909 syllabus, though a number of more vigorous movements and 'game-form' activities were included to invigorate and enliven the work. The small recreative section in the earlier syllabus was replaced by a chapter headed 'General Activity Exercises' which it was anticipated the children would find the most enjoyable part of the lesson. To encourage games further a supplement entitled *Suggestions in Regard to Games* was issued separately, as was an additional chapter dealing with the physical training of children under seven. To make the lessons less formal, 'general activity exercises' or 'game-like exercises' were to be introduced as breaks to relieve 'the restraint imposed by formal exercises on the natural desire for full movement'. It was still, however, considered necessary to include order exercises and movements as before, with class formations in ranks and files. It was a pious hope that the additional injunctions such as 'turning right and left with a jump' (as a game) and 'astride jumping—begin! Stop! '(informal) would add a dimension of enjoyment for children. Certainly the syllabus was the most comprehensive issued to date, for it included a wealth of material (seventy-two tables) and a deal of sensible advice to to help teachers in the practical situation in schools. It was a vast improvement upon its predecessor, but whether or not it had made the work sufficiently attractive to arouse the interest and enthusiasm of the children remained to be seen.

THE EFFECT UPON CHILDREN'S LIVES

What did the changes described in this chapter mean in terms of the school life of children, particularly poor children? At the Quayside school in Norwich drill was begun in 1902, in the context of large numbers arriving at school ill-shod, ill-clad and undernourished. Voluntary workers supplied some free meals in 1905 for the poorest children, and more meals were supplied as the result of the new Act of 1906. Interest in exercises was maintained by periodic visits of inspection. Organised games in the playground began in 1907, a fives court was built in the following year, and in 1909 the boys of the top two standards walked to Mousehold Heath to play football on one afternoon a week. In 1910 the introduction of medical inspections marked a major advance, but the eradication of dirt, disease and undernourishment was a long process. During World War I the health and general state of the boys was stated to be satisfactory, though the last three winters of the war brought an unsurpassed amount of ill health. In 1919 over 400 boys were being taught in eight classes in premises which were to be condemned as unfit for a school in 1925. What could be achieved by the teachers to create an environment suitable for the education of their charges was being done; the best use was being made of the rooms; the spirit in the school was good; its achievements included a high standard in music, and the children's interest in their schoolwork was reflected in their voluntary completion of homework. Plainly though, much remained to be done to create conditions suitable for the education of the sons of heroes.

COMPARATIVE DEVELOPMENTS IN PHYSICAL EDUCATION
1902–19

The fact that the greater attention paid to physical education towards the end of the nineteenth century in Germany was associated with nationalist and militarist policies was noted in the previous chapter. The turn of the century saw the continuation of this emphasis upon the production of 'virile generations'. There was in addition an intensification of the conflict between traditional gymnastics (*Turnen*) and sport. The *Turners* remained aggressively nationalist in outlook, rejecting the internationalist influences being propagated by the supporters of the revived Olympic games. Progressive elements had hived off from the parent association to form a separate Workers Gymnastics and Sports Association in 1896, and three years later a further split occurred when more reactionary members formed the *Deutsche Turnerbund*, an organisation noted for its racist views and strong anti-semitism. The growth of sport in the community was so inexorable that the *Turners* were forced to broaden their programmes by including sporting activities, though they endeavoured to stress the importance of a true German 'spirit' in their work.

Even such an anti-authoritarian movement as the *Wandervögel* was not free from association with nationalism and anti-semitism. State policy was to promote patriotic youth movements, united in 1911 in the Young Germany League directed by Field Marshal von Golz. The aim of this organisation was stated clearly: 'to strive through systematised physical training to strengthen the nationalist spirit in German youth', and it fostered its ideals among students, schoolboys and its affiliated societies.[31] Consequently by the outbreak of World War I physical education in Germany had lost its links with liberal thought, and had become an instrument of the authoritarian state with the role of preparing youth for military service.

In contrast with Germany, both Sweden and Denmark reveal during these years a lessening of military influence in school gymnastics. In Denmark, school gymnastics were separated from military gymnastics and placed under a civilian inspector, K. A. Knudsen, in 1904. Another important step towards developing the work upon sound scientific lines was the establishment of a laboratory at the University of Copenhagen under

Dr J. Lindhard, who conducted investigations into the physiology of exercise as applied both to gymnastics and to work. Similarly in Sweden, the character of gymnastics was altered beneficially, especially as the result of the innovations of Elin Falk and Elli Björksten in the programme for women and young children. In both countries, too, there was a rapid expansion of sports and games, provisions for which were urged by the national governments. In 1897 a National Committee was established in Denmark to develop games in schools, while the various sports associations in Sweden combined in 1903 to form the Swedish Sports Federation, a National Sports Badge being introduced a few years later.

Similarly in the United States the early years of the century saw the increased interest in sport in the community reflected in the general expansion of physical education in the schools. The acceptance of developmental theories according play an essential role in physical growth also had the effect of giving an educational stimulus to the growth of games and the provision of playgrounds. Increase in concern for the health and medical care of schoolchildren was contemporaneous with that in the United Kingdom. During the first decade of the century interest was stimulated by the White House Conference on School Health as a consequence of which dental and medical inspection and the treatment of defective vision and hearing were introduced more widely. Gradually, too, the schools accepted responsibility for the care and training of defective children. Curti points out the arguments that were used to justify this extension of the school's activity:

> ... it was argued that social maladjustments now made it impossible to thrust the entire responsibility for the health of children on parents. It was also pointed out that the rapid urbanisation of American life required school to assume many of the functions that could safely be left to nature in a simpler society.[32]

Other supporters of intervention were the anti-alcohol crusaders and those who associated the lack of playgrounds and swimming pools with the development of anti-social behaviour which formed the basis of later crime.

The growing emphasis upon the social purposes of education, whose leading proponent was John Dewey, also had the effect of emphasising the increased importance of physical education by adding social and moral objectives to those of better health. The stress upon educational objectives, with better health being regarded as a by-product of physical activity rather than its primary aim, resulted in dissatisfaction with German and Swedish gymnastics and with the advocacy of a more broadly based programme, a reflection of which was the spread of summer camps.[33] By 1918 the enactment of compulsory-attendance legislation meant that the vast majority of American children attended elementary schools, though as in England, the employment of child labour, especially in the factories and shops of the cities, remained an unsolved problem.[34]

7

The influences affecting physical education in the schools 1919–45

. . . it appears not improbable that nearly half the population of England and Wales subsists, to a greater or lesser extent, below the safety line of nutrition.

G. C. M. M'Gonigle and J. Kirby,
Poverty and Public Health (1933)

What is needed is more consideration, encouragement and support from the Authorities, *better provision, more playing fields, more and better swimming baths, etc. As physical culture becomes more fully recognised as an integral part of a liberal education, the less shall we need formal and corrective work in physical training,* and the less we shall need medical treatment.

The Chief Medical Officer of the
Board of Education (1928)

Social conditions between the wars determined the development both of sport in society and of physical education in the schools. The dominating root influence was that of economic depression. Unemployment (including the unemployment of adolescents) and poverty became the major social problems. The number of unemployed reached two million in 1921, to rise even higher later and to remain above the one million mark until after the outbreak of World War II. It did not affect the whole country equally; most hard hit were the north and Wales, areas dependent upon the basic heavy industries. For those in work there were steady improvements in real wages and living standards. Advances in science and technology exacerbated the contrast between those in need and other sections of the community and also the contrast between areas.[1] The foundations for the growth of sport and recreation had been laid, and among those with increased money and opportunity there was a remarkable growth of interest and participation in sport and in a range of physical recreation. To relieve the demoralising effect of long-term unemployment, charitable and voluntary agencies, supported by a number of influential people, worked to provide sporting facilities. This work was left to private agencies because public spending was curtailed drastically when the re-stocking boom of 1919–20 turned abruptly to a slump. The government wielded the 'Geddes axe' to pare expenditure on a wide scale in 1921 and the education programme was affected severely, Day Continuation schools being an early casualty. There was a partial recovery but in 1929 the country plunged into a depression of hitherto unknown severity, reaching its climax in the financial crisis of 1931 which led to a further round of cuts in government expenditure. The bottom was reached in 1932–3, the slow process of recovery being initiated in the following year.

DEVELOPMENTS UNDER FINANCIAL STRINGENCY

Despite the depression the period reveals a remarkable development of interest in recreation in the open air. Picnics and rambles became popular weekend pastimes in the early post-war years. For many the advent of the cheap mass-produced motor car increased the opportunity, while for those unable to afford the luxury of their own transport there were the new suburban bus routes and cheap excursions by train. Sunbathing became highly fashionable in the late twenties and almost all sport gained markedly in popularity, especially swimming and association football. The provision of swimming baths and cheap excursions to the sea made learning to swim a possibility, whilst almost every village had its football team competing in the local league. In South Wales and the north of England respective versions of rugby football were preferred to soccer, though often the two codes co-existed, sometimes even using the same village pitch! A cult of slimming amongst the upper classes was a feature of the late twenties—an ironic preoccupation in view of the millions on 'short commons'—some devotees incorporating physical exercises into their endeavours. But the 'keep fit' movement was far more ubiquitous; centred initially in the north-east and London, it spread rapidly, especially through the Women's League of Health & Beauty. The movement contributed to the climax in the national campaign for physical fitness launched in 1936.

During this period physical education in the schools was firmly established under the aegis of the School Medical Service, its development on a therapeutic basis being guided firmly by the Chief Medical Officer. Throughout the inter-war years work in the schools was handicapped by shortage of money, and schemes for extending educational opportunities for the adolescent were an early casualty.[2] Despite annual exhortations the great majority of local authorities were unwilling to appoint organisers of physical education to develop the work in their areas; facilities in the majority of schools were completely inadequate and there was a dire shortage of trained staff. There was a naïve retention of the belief that physical education (which had the inestimable value of being cheap) could play a major role in preventive medicine. Certainly this was the justification urged by the Chief Medical Officer for the maintenance and development of physical activities in schools. The view of the radicals was that this was merely a cheap palliative for more fundamental (and more expensive) remedies for malnutrition and disease, but one which was politically acceptable, whereas more realistic social policies were not.

The content of the work was based upon the official syllabuses of 1919 and 1933. The attempt was made to superimpose 'progressive' educational ideas upon the underlying basis of therapeutic exercises, whose yardstick of assessment was the evaluation of posture. The Chief Medical Officer in his report for 1920 urged the need to consider the importance of the individual, to consider the physical and mental well-being of the child and to realise the significance of play. An addendum to the report described the revision of work for young children by Elin Falk at Stockholm and Elli Björksten's development of women's gymnastics. The general principles of these progressive methods were less stereotyped and less formal approaches, a stress upon full, simple movements and the condemnation of 'position drill' as of little value in the correction of malposture and poor physique. Rhythmic exercise and the differentiation of men's and women's work were encouraged. Of primary importance was the spirit of the work: ' "Gladje", a word equivalent to "joie de vivre", is the keynote of the teaching and is essential to physical and mental well-being.' Attention was drawn also to the developments in men's work of Niels Bukh at the Folk High School at Ollerup, where continuous rhythmic movements and vigour were emphasised. Bukh brought his gymnastic teams to give displays in England from 1927 onwards and his methods were imitated widely.

The stress upon a widely based programme of physical activities 'devised in a broad and catholic spirit' was reiterated in the 1933 syllabus. Not only were physical gains to be considered, but also the beneficial influences upon mind and character. For younger children the value of free movement in the form of play was emphasised, whilst throughout the school years the recreative aspect and enjoyment of the work were to be regarded as of the greatest importance. Linked with this outlook was the retention of the belief in systematic exercise which could be judged by the standards of good posture. Concern for posture had grown over the years, being influenced by a number of external developments. The science of industrial psychology had emanated from the Health of Munitions Workers' Committee (1915–17), whose work had been continued by the Industrial Fatigue Board supported by the Medical Research Council.[3] In investigating industrial efficiency and the health of workers the importance of posture in relation to the onset of fatigue had been emphasised. Interest in the academic aspects of the evolution of posture had been stirred by Sir Arthur Keith's lectures in 1923.[4] The preoccupation of the physical-education profession with posture gathered momentum in the succeeding decades, being reflected in investigations into the frequency of postural defects, in the establishment of posture classes for remedial work and by evaluating a range of activities by their benefits in terms of posture standards. The intensity of the concentration upon the subject can be estimated from the amount of space allocated to physical development and spinal deformity in the 1938 Report of the Spens Committee, whose brief was to consider the organisation of secondary education and especially the functions of grammar and technical schools.

The Chief Medical Officer was deeply concerned with the disparity between the standard of work in the more progressive areas and the rest of the country, considering the key to progress to be the appointment by the local education authorities of physical-education organisers to initiate, co-ordinate and inspire the work in their areas. Yet he was unable to win over many local authorities. In 1920 organisers were employed in only 79 of the 316 local authorities, and in the prevailing economic climate there seemed little chance of a rapid increase in their numbers. Dr George Newman used his annual reports to give an account of an organiser's duties and to urge the local authorities to retain existing staff or to make new appointments. In 1928, assessing what changes had been accomplished, he saw the authorities' reluctance to act reflected in 'slow and inadequate' progress in the work. He found much to praise in the efforts of the elementary-school teachers, despite little support from their employers in the provision of equipment and facilities, but regretted that little progress had been made in the municipal secondary schools. He urged the authorities to view expenditure upon facilities as preferable to expenditure upon medical care. This need to stress value for money and to defend existing commitments recurred in 1930–1 when the nation suffered another acute financial crisis. The School Medical Service in this year accounted for 5 per cent of the outlay on elementary education, while the organisation of physical training cost a total of £64,294. By 1933, Newman's last year in office, only 107 authorities employed organisers, and despite increased national interest in physical recreation and the wave of enthusiasm in the schools which followed the publication of the 1933 syllabus, the number had risen only to 124 by January 1936.[5] It has to be remembered that the authorities had to make cuts on a wide front, delaying their plans to reorganise their elementary schools and to build new central and secondary schools.

Specialist courses were also victims of the need for economy. The only course for the training of men specialists for work in secondary schools and as organisers, that at Sheffield under H. A. Cole, was closed in 1923. The course at Reading University College for women intending to specialise in continuative education was also terminated.[6] The voluntary colleges for women (neither the colleges nor the students were grant-aided), continued to train middle-class girls for posts in the grammar, high and independent schools and for lecturing and organising work, but until 1933 there was nowhere in England where men could be trained. A small number were trained in Scotland and in Denmark, where courses with English as the medium of instruction were established. A survey by Captain Grenfell, H.M. Staff Inspector for Physical Training, of boys' secondary schools in 1923 revealed that 80 per cent of the staff were inefficiently trained; indeed many schools used former army instructors. Vacation courses were begun at Scarborough in 1924 and at Eastbourne in 1925, aided in the latter year by the grant of maintenance allowances for students. A *Reference Book of Gymnastic Training for Boys* was published in 1927, intended to help these teachers with a cursory training to teach with reasonable efficiency.

THE SYLLABUS OF PHYSICAL TRAINING, 1933

A stimulus to reorganisation of schools came from the Hadow Report, *The Education of the Adolescent*, published in 1926. It recommended the end of the socially stigmatised 'elementary' school and its replacement by 'primary' education to the age of eleven, and by the recognition of all subsequent education as 'secondary'. The expansion of existing secondary (grammar) schools was advocated, with the development of other types of post-primary schools for which the name 'modern' schools was suggested. To meet the needs of the reorganised schools the *Syllabus of Physical Training* was revised, and was intended mainly for use in primary schools. Again the dual aims of the work—postural and educational—were stated, the methods being systematic exercise and 'a liberal education in games and sports'. New exercises designed for the 'special encouragement of good posture and flexibility of muscles and joints' were included, while the establishment of remedial classes was advocated. Also included was a lengthy section describing games and activities suitable for the playground which could be regarded as preparatory training for the skills of major games.

Teachers found this syllabus an invaluable, practical working aid. The table of exercises was simple and there was a wealth of teaching material included. The illustrations, showing children actively engaged in work of a high standard, were inspirational, setting an example which many in the less progressive areas or schools attempted to emulate. Progressive teachers used the syllabus as a base for advance, but inevitably—as in all works of this kind—its very comprehensiveness and thoroughness resulted in the majority of teachers regarding it as the complete answer. This meant that many teachers who used and relied upon the syllabus in the 1930s were resistant to change when later new methods were presented for their consideration.

The syllabus was received with great enthusiasm in the more progressive areas, there being an unprecedented demand from teachers for courses based upon the activities included in it, while organisers reported the zealous response of the children to the increased freedom and wider scope of the work. The emphasis upon posture was reinforced after 1933 when the children's actual physique was revealed when first they stripped for exercise. Organisers made the most of the opportunity afforded by the introduction of the new syllabus to make an impact upon the schools. In London, for example, 12,000 free copies were distributed, thirty-eight meetings of head teachers were held to explain the work, 1,583 teachers attended courses and another 901 attended demonstrations, yet it was 'quite impossible to cope with the demand'. The authority granted a special requisition to improve the stock of games equipment, and demonstration lessons by classes of children were attended by members of the Education Committee, His Majesty's Inspectors and the School Medical Officers.[7] The organisers welcomed the inclusion of recreative activities and team games. To some of them, their work in seeing that teachers had achieved competence in teaching the exercises of the 1919 syllabus had seemed too redolent of 'gradgrind'. They were also strongly aware that the best part of the Swedish system was not being applied to the mass of children. The junior schools lacked the apparatus on which children could hang and swing and little could be done to repair the omission of suspension exercises. In the poorer parts of the country it was also only too evident that a proportion of children were in no condition to benefit from exercise—working with badly nourished children in playground sheds in wintry conditions when a fair proportion had wet feet because they were badly shod was not conducive to the generation of great enthusiasm. They made advances where they could.

THE PHYSICAL CONDITION OF THE CHILDREN 1919–45

The School Medical Service sponsored physical education primarily for its contribution to the health of schoolchildren, therefore it is important to attempt to evaluate the progress made by the mid-1930s. The apparent gain in the cleanliness was remarkable, for 16 million examinations of individual children in 1934 revealed that fewer than 27 per 1,000 were dirty.[8] Revelations in World War II indicated, however, that this was a gross underestimation of the problem. The high incidence of verminous children among those evacuated caused real shock. Over 30 per cent of London children received in West Suffolk, and of Liverpool children received in Shrewsbury, for example, were infected.[9]

There was a great reservoir of infection in children under five and in girls over fourteen which had not been cleared by the measures taken in schools. Success had been achieved by the school doctors, chiefly by the use of X-ray treatment, in reducing very markedly the incidence of ringworm. Lowndes points out the social significance of this: the drastic reduction of this most troublesome disease removed the last valid obstacle to the patronage of the public elementary schools by middle-class parents.[10]

The annual statistics published by the Chief Medical Officer also showed improvements in the incidence of the diseases associated with childhood, compared with previous estimates, but contemporary investigators commented that this did not indicate a satisfactory state of affairs.[11] M'Gonigle and Kirby point out that detailed special examinations discovered a much higher incidence of physical defects than was revealed by routine medical inspections. They also showed that variations in standards for assessing defects in various parts of the country raised serious doubts of the validity of the statistics published by school medical officers:

> ... it would appear that tonsils, adenoids, and tonsils and adenoids [assessed under separate headings], requiring treatment are twelve times more common in Sunderland than in Tynemouth, while Swindon is in the fortunate position of having only one-twenty-third the cases occurring in Sunderland which have to be kept under observation.

M'Gonigle and Kirby showed that nutrition was the dominant factor in public health and that faulty nutrition was primarily due to poverty. Again, investigations using stated criteria showed a higher incidence of malnutrition, and that rachitic stigmata were more prevalent in schoolchildren than the medical officers' reports indicated. A detailed consideration of economic, environmental and social conditions led them to conclude that, on the basis of the British Medical Association minimum diets, probably nearly half the population of England and Wales lived below the safety level of nutrition. This estimate was confirmed by Boyd Orr's investigation to show the consumption of food at different income levels. Using an optimum physiological standard he estimated that 4·5 million people were deficient in every dietary constituent, 9 millions deficient in vitamins and minerals generally, and a further 9 million deficient in several of the important vitamins and minerals.[12] Whereas routine medical inspection showed 23·9 per 1,000 children suffering from malnutrition in 1933, special surveys found that the proportion was 79 per 1,000, while M'Gonigle and Kirby, noting the unscientific connotation of the term 'malnutrition', imply that in the depressed areas it seemed likely that some 25 per cent of the children were affected by malnutrition in some degree.[13]

The provision of school meals had been affected by the drive for economy. The industrial unrest of the years immediately following World War I had made it necessary to give far more school meals: during 1920–1 12 million were supplied as opposed to something over 6 million the previous year. The closure of the mines had required the introduction of special methods in the affected areas, such as Rhondda and Durham.[14] In 1921–2 over 60 million meals were provided at a total gross cost of £983,182, but the government restricted future expenditure in any year to £300,000, rationing the money to local authorities. In evaluating nutritional standards the Chief Medical Officer came to the general conclusion that the 'general health and physique of school-children is at least as good now as it was before the war', though some local authority school medical officers, such as Dr Newsholme of the North Riding and Dr Chetwood of Sheffield, disagreed from evidence in their areas. The Chief Medical Officer also sought consolation from the fact that £300,000 would still feed 'a large number of children'. His reports for 1923 and 1924 reveal that the fall in agricultural wages was being reflected in a decline in the physical condition of country children too. During the strikes of 1926 special measures had to be taken again; indeed for thirty weeks in the mining areas parents were without income, apart from public relief; during that year the total number of meals exceeded 70 million.[15] In 1931, to effect savings, it was insisted that children had to be poor and undernourished to qualify for subsidised meals. These, of the 'soup kitchen' variety, were usually served in drab central premises.

Milk had been supplied to children in need from 1921, and in 1934 a Milk Marketing Board scheme providing one-third of a pint of milk for a halfpenny was introduced. The cost of this scheme was £500,000 a year and it was part of a national campaign to increase milk consumption. The attitude that these measures of alleviation were sufficient, provoked a Labour MP, W. G. Cove, to remark bitterly a few years later, 'I am beginning to think that the public conscience is being drowned as far as nutrition is concerned by a third of a pint of milk a day. Nutrition means variety as well as milk.'[16]

It seems evident too that officialdom underplayed the impact of increased unemployment upon adolescents. The abandonment of the principle of compulsion in the establishment of Day Continuation schools has been noted already. Investigations revealed that unemployment had exacerbated gravely the problems of school-leavers. A detailed inquiry by Eager and Secretan in Bermondsey in 1925 revealed that unemployment was much more extensive than shown in the official figures. They estimated that there were some 120,000 unemployed boys between the ages of fourteen and eighteen in London alone. They described the lasting deterioration, moral and physical, resulting from unemployment during these critical years, and castigated the makeshift nature of the provision made in the Juvenile Employment Centres.[17] The Hadow Report of 1926 attempted to make distinctive provision in schools for older children, by making the division between primary and secondary education at the age of eleven, and by advocating for 'non-academic' children an education with a strong practical bias during their last two years. Reorganisation of the schools proceeded slowly, money remaining short, and there were formidable obstacles to be faced in the rural areas and in overcoming denominational objections. However, the basic problems of the wastage due to the unselective employment of school-leavers and the evils accompanying adolescent unemployment remained unsolved.

GROWTH OF PHYSICAL RECREATION IN THE COMMUNITY

During the inter-war years the growth of interest in physical recreation in the community was sponsored by voluntary organisations enjoying the patronage of influential and wealthy people. The National Council of Social Service, formed in 1919 to co-ordinate the expected major advances in the provision of social welfare, played an active role in encouraging and aiding a wide variety of voluntary organisations. The presidency of the Duke of York and the patronage of an impressive list of supporters ensured the success of the National Playing Fields Association formed in 1925 to improve the provision of games facilities. Physical recreation and physical fitness were being viewed as palliatives for the economic and social results of the depression. As Newman wrote, 'The almost feverish devotion to health was, in a sense, an escape from some of the grim realities of the industrial depression.' Prominent men and women gave freely of their time and money to aid philanthropic enterprises benefiting working-class children. The National Association of Boys' Clubs found 'leaders were good publicity and a good propaganda for ideas ... [in addition] ... the Presidency of the Duke of Gloucester bestowed status'. The chairman of the association during its critical formative period was J. Heron Eccles, a prominent Liverpool businessman, its treasurer Sir Edward Campbell, MP.[18]

The Youth Hostels Association, formed in 1930, had as its first president G. M. Trevelyan, who formed an important link between the new association and the National Trust. Trevelyan was an excellent example of those (according to Professor Macintosh) 'far-seeing men and women of an older group who were quick to appreciate the health values . . . of the cult of the open air'. He saw that youth hostels would bring

... strenuous open-air holidays within the scope of many thousands of pedestrians and cyclists, young men and women, most of them from the great cities in which the Industrial Revolution had shut off the bulk of the population from rural sights and sounds. . . . Holidays in the country are a mitigation of this evil and a source of spiritual power and joy which must affect both directly and indirectly all the activities of the coming age.[19]

The youth hostels were based upon the remarkable success of the *Jugend-herbergen* movement in post-war Germany. Other prominent supporters included Sir Patrick Abercrombie and Archbishop Temple. Trevelyan's voluntary work began with the National Trust in the 1920s and later he was one of the founders of the Outward Bound Movement. The need for a co-ordinating body for the numerous voluntary organisations engaged in developing physical activities was met in 1935 by the creation of the Central Council of Recreative Physical Training, supported by royal patronage and by a formidable number of people prominent in national life. Charitable trusts such as the Carnegie Trust, the King George's Jubilee Trust and the King George Memorial Fund also provided valuable assistance.

THE NEW PRIORITY FOR PHYSICAL EDUCATION 1935-9

Government interest in physical education in the schools received a remarkable fillip in 1936. The dramatic change of emphasis was exemplified by the promotion of physical education from the status of a few lines in the section devoted to the School Medical Service to the entire first chapter in the Report of the Board of Education for 1936-7 and 1937-8. Chuter Ede's attribution of this to the example set in the dictatorships of Italy and Germany of concentrated attention on the physical training of the young seems well justified.[20] The Board issued *Circular 1445* in January 1936 as a statement of its policy for physical education in schools and for youth during the post-school period. In it the school programme was viewed as the basis of physical fitness in the adolescent years. The national policy was to encourage developments at every stage. In the elementary schools there should be the equivalent of a daily period of physical education, three periods a week of gymnastics and physical exercises, and time for games and swimming. Playing fields were to be provided for the elementary schools and gymnasia and playing fields for the secondary and technical schools. For the post-school period there was to be no imitation of the 'centralised methods in use in some continental countries', but reliance upon 'enthusiasm and initiative' of local authorities and voluntary organisations. The supply of teachers of physical education was to be increased and vacation courses were to be set up to meet the need for youth leaders with knowledge of physical training. Authorities were urged to regard the appointment of organisers as an 'indispensable' part of the provision for physical education. The syllabus of 1933 was to be supplemented by publications suitable for the post-school years.

This then was the 'national plan' for the development of physical fitness in schools, the basis of much progress during the following three years. The number of organisers increased markedly, so that in 1939 there were only sixty-three authorities without any. Proposals for 199 gymnasia and for 8,450 acres of playing fields for elementary schools had been approved, and for 244 gymnasia, 20 swimming baths and 2,006 acres of playing fields for secondary schools, with an additional 43 gymnasia for technical schools.[21] Some authorities made elaborate provision to overcome their difficulties: in London classrooms were built on playing-field sites so that children might be kept at the same place for a whole day to shorten the distances travelled; it was intended to ensure that every child in the city aged from ten to fifteen would play games on a grass field once a week, and spend one whole day in open country.[22] Specialist courses in physical education for men were begun at Loughborough College in 1935 and at Goldsmith's College in 1937. Advanced courses were initiated in ten men's and seventeen women's colleges, and also special intensive courses of three months' duration. During 1939 it was stated officially:

Physical education ... is now an established part of the curriculum of all the schools within the purview of the Board. Every child in these schools, unless medically exempt, receives regular instruction

in gymnastics and in one or more branches of physical education
. . . there has been built up in the elementary schools a physical
training, which, in scope and quality, need not fear comparison
with that which can be produced in any other country.[23]

To aid the government to make an objective assessment of 'the
national standard of physical efficiency' the British Medical Association established a Physical Education Committee which
reported in 1936. The result was a comprehensive condemnation
of the existing 'general neglect of bodily fitness'. In fact, as already
seen, great progress was made in the years immediately following
this report. Diet, it was stated roundly, was the chief factor at
issue: 'Since physical training increases metabolism, an addition
must be made to the diet of persons, especially unemployed
adolescents, whose nutrition is inadequate if any benefit is to be
derived from exercise.' It revealed the inadequacy of facilities in
the elementary schools; the neglect of physical education in the
junior technical schools; its low status in public schools; the inadequate allocation of time; the shortage of trained teachers; that
physical education was conspicuous by its absence in the universities; and the continuing reluctance of the local authorities to
appoint organisers. The committee advocated a large increase in
recreative facilities in order to improve the fitness of the adolescent population and made recommendations to improve the
deficiencies they found in the schools.

To meet the first of these needs the government issued (January
1937) a White Paper which formed the basis of the Physical Training and Recreation Act. The primary purpose was to supplement
the existing work and inadequate facilities. No compulsion was
envisaged, but aid was to be channelled through two National
Advisory Councils, one for England and Wales, the other for
Scotland, with two grant committees and a number of local committees, grants being based upon individual applications. It was
proposed also to set up a new National College of Physical Training for the training of youth leaders.

The government's intention was to keep the debate of the bill apart from any discussion of the effectiveness of the measures being taken to alleviate malnutrition in the population. Opposition MPs, however, were not easily side-tracked. In Mr Lees-Smith's opinion:

> ... the greatest single stride which could be taken towards the improvement of the physique of the nation would be to keep children out of the mills, factories and mines until their bodies are fully developed. .... Until the problem of nutrition is solved, proposals which are merely for physical training will be built upon a foundation of feebleness, anaemia and debility.[24]

Others supported this view, while James Maxton expressed the enlightened opinion that physical activity ought to be encouraged for the pleasure it gave, and that health ought to be its by-product, not the main objective. He also described the utter inadequacy of schools in the industrial areas, suggesting that no plans for new schools be approved unless adequate provision were made for sports and games.[25] In moving the second reading of the bill Mr Oliver Stanley dwelt at length upon the physical and therapeutic benefits which would result from an increase in recreation. A diffuse and rambling debate followed, the most trenchant contribution coming from Aneurin Bevan who considered that the 'whole subject apart from one or two speeches seems to have been debated in a vacuum. Everybody considers physical training to be quite removed from the economic and social background of those who are to be trained'. He condemned Stanley's vindication of the bill for the benefits to be derived, and he condemned too the motives for the encouragement of physical training in schools as a 'miserable substitute' for providing sufficient playgrounds.[26]

The Act allocated £2,000,000 to be spent over three years and thereafter expenditure at the rate of £150,000 a year. By March 1939 grants for £1,500,000 had been approved, though 'only £532,982 had actually been spent when war broke out in 1939, and of this sum £152,957 had gone on salaries and administrative expenses'.[27] Youth organisations did not view the National Fitness Council with unqualified approval:

Despite the many facilities which the National Fitness Council offered it was regarded with considerable suspicion by the youth organisations, partly because of its emphasis on physical, presumably as opposed to moral, fitness, and partly because the scale on which it worked was over-grandiose for the modest needs and ambitions of the majority of the organisations.[28]

THE EFFECT OF WORLD WAR II UPON PHYSICAL EDUCATION

During the war physical education suffered, in the words of the Chief Medical Officer, 'a severe regression'. Organisers and teachers joined the forces, some areas being severely denuded. The specialist men's courses were closed, as were most vacation courses though those at Loughborough were able to continue.[29] The drive to develop the 'Service of Youth', however, which required boys and girls to register at sixteen, when they were encouraged to join a youth organisation, inaugurated a great expansion of youth work, especially in the pre-service organisation. To aid this, the release of organisers and physical education teachers who exercised the option was sanctioned in 1940. Many games facilities were of course requisitioned or evacuated, both indoor accommodation and playing fields being affected; during the earlier years of the war swimming pools became almost non-existent, though an improvement occurred after 1943. Schools were much affected, and in many the loss of showers and the lack of kit meant a lowering of hygienic standards. Out-of-school activities and fixtures were curtailed, while evacuated schools had only makeshift arrangements.

The results of a national food policy which involved the first large-scale application of the science of nutrition to the population, and the treatment of children as a priority class, had beneficial results. School feeding was reduced drastically during the first twelve months of the war, but in 1941 a complete School Meals Service was initiated. One of the results of bombing was to make large-scale communal feeding necessary, and the government saw the importance of supplementing children's rations by the provision of school meals.[30] By the end of the war nearly 2 million children were having school dinners and over 70 per cent of schoolchildren were having milk at school daily. As a result, the Chief Medical Officer reported there was 'no positive evidence' of a decline in the health and physique of children during the war years; indeed available evidence indicated that their nutrition had almost certainly improved.[31] It was the first time that the physical care of children had become of truly national concern and importance:

> It was the revelations of evacuation in 1939 and the profound stirrings of national unity in the crisis of 1940 that finally brought the two Englands together and caused even the least discerning to appreciate the worst of which social neglect was capable.[32]

The arrival of children who were verminous, ill fed, ill clad and ill shod in the reception areas caused a profound reaction.[33] Wartime conditions, including 'shelter-living', led to the recurrence of vermin infection on a large scale, an abrupt rise in the incidence of scabies and an increase in ringworm.[34]

Evacuation made evident not only the consequences of social neglect but also the inadequacies of an elementary-school system reorganised on a piecemeal basis. Educational deficiencies, especially on the technical side, were revealed. There were '. . . many gaps to be filled if the service was to be established on positive educational principles and no longer depend on what wealthy communities were willing to spend and what poor communities could afford.'[35]

The 1944 Act confirmed the responsibility of the local authorities for the physical care of children. It was their duty to provide milk and meals, employing a meals organiser to ensure an efficient service. Authorities had the duty, too, of providing adequate facilities for primary, secondary and further education, now considered as a continuous, progressive system. The school-leaving age was to be raised to fifteen and at some future date part-time day attendance at County Colleges was to become compulsory for all those who left school before eighteen—as after World War I, however, this provision for adolescents was not implemented.

Most local authorities did not take advantage of the opportunity offered them of creating a scheme of secondary education based upon equality of opportunity; the grammar schools had the better qualified staff, better accommodation for many years, and retained a prestigious position. Standards in physical education were, however, made uniform, so that there was no discrimination in the provision of playing fields, gymnasiums and swimming baths;[36] eventually, after the implementation of a school-building programme over many years, this resulted in many working-class children being afforded the opportunity of taking part in a full programme of physical activities. The Act also made it a duty of authorities to provide adequate means for recreation and physical training for the post-school population, and transferred the financial aids set up under the Physical Training and Recreation Act of 1937 to the newly created Ministry of Education. Another significant administrative change was made in 1945, when the oversight of physical education was transferred from the Chief Medical Officer to the Senior Chief Inspector of Schools. The era of therapeutic physical education was drawing to a close.

In any evaluation of physical education in the schools during these years the marked contrast between the penny-pinching support from the authorities before 1936 and the generous scale of the aid available after that date stands out. Despite the firm leadership of Sir George Newman the majority of the local authorities were unable or unwilling to implement the policy advocated until 1936. In referring to Newman's inability to get health education across to the schools despite prodigious efforts in the 1920s Professor Mackintosh concludes 'he was before his time'.[37] In his drive to develop physical education in the schools he seems also to have been fighting almost alone. This was reflected in the glaring disparity between the standard of work in the more progressive areas and the rest, Newman stating in his report for 1933 that 'some of the unorganised areas are a generation behind the most advanced'. It is important not to base an estimate of the work done in schools purely upon descriptions of what happened in the more favoured areas, and to remember the dichotomy which existed in social conditions in the country during these years.

Viewing elementary schools in 1938, F. H. Spencer considered that four-fifths of the buildings needed to be destroyed and replaced. Of physical education he wrote:

> Five years ago it would have been true to say that no elementary school had a gymnasium. But while Denmark and other truly democratic countries ensure that physical education can be efficiently carried on, we do not. There may now be (though I doubt it) twenty elementary schools (out of 30,000) in England and Wales with the facilities for physical education always provided for the middle-class child. There are no more.[38]

Spencer blamed the lack of first-class leadership at the Board of Education and the lack of sympathy of permanent officials with working-class education. Certainly the attitude that public education was a form of national charity persisted. The broadened basis of physical education in the schools, actively supported by government aid after 1936, was undoubtedly influenced by the growth of recreation and the 'cult of the open air' in society as a whole. But the major problem in education in 1919 had been to meet the educational and physical needs of the post-school generation and to prevent the wastage of the benefits of national education. This problem remained unsolved; indeed the 1944 Education Act's measures for continuative education remain unimplemented.

COMPARATIVE DEVELOPMENTS IN CONTINENTAL COUNTRIES
AND THE USA

In Germany in the inter-war years great attention was paid to sport and the cult of the open air. A parallel development in the schools resulted in physical education acquiring an elevated status. The immediate reason was the need to counteract the effects of four years of war upon the children and, in particular, to remedy the serious problem of malnutrition, the result of blockade. Support for physical activities also came from those who saw them as an antidote to the over-intellectualised education of the past and as suited to democratic ideals. The Weimar republic was concerned to extend opportunities for physical recreation to the mass of the population as part of a broadly based programme of social reform. Many municipalities embarked upon extensive programmes of public works in which facilities for sport and recreation featured prominently. Each major city built a large sports stadium during the decade after the war, the most famous being that at Cologne, which was opened in 1923. Many of the ideas developed by the government were those of Carl Diem, who was responsible too for the introduction, with resounding success, of the German Sports Badge, on the Swedish model. The Reich School Conference of 1920 urged the development of physical education and official action included the foundation in 1920 of the Deutsche Hochschule für Leibesübungen in Berlin, where teachers' courses of a high standard were developed, making use of the magnificent facilities. Elementary schools in Prussia had three compulsory periods of physical education per week, with four in the secondary schools, similar regulations being imposed in the other German states.

There were some fears that physical education and sport would encourage a spirit of aggression and become associated with nationalist, anti-democratic and racist sentiments. The League of Radical School Reformers urged that physical education should be encouraged only as part of a progressive social policy, and that the work in gymnastics should be liberalised by an emphasis upon rhythmic movement and the aesthetic aspect. A number of individual versions of rhythmic-gymnastics were developed, seen as a counter to the rigidity of *Turnen* and to the growth of the cult of sport in the community. In certain schools, however, for example the small number of State Prussian boarding schools and the Salem schools founded by Prince Max of Baden, the military ideal was very strongly upheld. Though such developments were exceptional, Grunberger indicates the role played by the schools in general as incubators of nationalism during the Weimar period.[39] Outside the schools, the youth organisations attached to political movements, such as the German National Party and Stahlhelm—anti-democratic, nationalist and militarist in outlook —vigorously pursued sports activities as an integral part of the programme.

The importance attached by the Nazis to physical fitness and to the physical preparation of the population for war is well known. In the schools physical education was accorded a prime importance, the time allotted being increased in 1935 and in 1937, when a daily period was made mandatory; in school reports the subject was given pride of place. A large number of advisory posts in physical education was created, and the support of teachers for the regime can be seen from the large numbers from the profession who rose to prominence in the party hierarchy. Within the schools the status of the physical education teacher was raised. In the Nazi elite schools—the SS-governed 'Napolas' and the Adolf Hitler schools where the chief criteria for enrolment were party sponsorship and physical prowess—physical activities were designed to develop the attributes essential to fighting soldiers. Fitness and physical hardness were developed by strenuous programmes of activity, with prolonged and arduous military-type manoeuvres as periodic tests of toughness and stamina. A similar stress upon physical fitness and aggression was applied to the post-school adolescent. All sporting clubs and organisations were brought under direct state or party control under von Tschammer und Osten, the Reich sports leader. In close collaboration were the youth movements, the Hitler Youth and the *Deutsches Jungvolk*, each with its own strenuous programme of physical activities, tested at various levels by sports badges.

The total result of such concentrated attention was the creation of a vast scheme of physical training under the panoply of the state, one based upon a perverted idealism ignoble in its aims and extreme in its methods. The climax of the training scheme was achieved in war games with live ammunition in which fatal casualties were acceptable. If physical education is defined as contributing to the total education of a civilised man, then the Nazi scheme cannot be classified as such. Inevitably there was a decline in intellectual standards in German schools as the result of the emphasis upon developing physical toughness and inculcating corrupt moral values.

In contrast, Denmark and Sweden illustrate the development of physical education by using advances in the scientific knowledge of the effect of exercise, and on the basis of liberalising developments in educational thought and practice. The social context was that of a democratic society which made provision for the medical inspection and care of the population, including a comprehensive scheme of medical care in the schools. In both countries sport and activities in the open air were encouraged, particularly in summer; and in winter increasing facilities were available for community participation in gymnastics, which had the support accorded to a national sport. The establishment of indoor and outdoor facilities on a large scale, to provide for a range of interests, in the Copenhagen Sports Park in 1911 was an interesting pioneering innovation, followed by a number of similar developments. Increased participation in sport in both countries was encouraged by the sports-badge programme.

In the schools the gymnastics programme was based upon Ling's exercises, modified as the result of Lindhardt's experimental work and developed into progressive classified systems by K. A. Knudsen in Denmark and J. G. Thulin in Sweden. Both these men stressed the value of 'all-round harmonious' physical development and the contribution of physical education to the total education of the child. Separate programmes for girls and young children were developed on 'movement gymnastic' lines from the original contribution of Elin Falk, Maja Carlquist, Elli Björksten and Agnete Bertram. Men's gymnastics was revitalised as the result of Niels Bukh's work at the Folk High School at Ollerup from 1919. Bukh emphasised vigorous rhythmical movements in impressive sequences of linked movements. His demonstrations influenced boys' gymnastics to some degree, but his methods were most widely adopted in adult clubs and in the folk high schools.

Developments in the United States during this period illustrate the way in which social pressures govern the course of development of physical education. This was a time of marked and sustained expansion in educational provision. There was a general acceptance of the principle that a democracy must provide more and better education as the foundation of furthering equality of opportunity. In the immediate years after World War I concern for child health and welfare was an aspect of this orientation towards the social purposes of education, other features of which were concern for education in citizenship, for the 'Americanisation' of the children of immigrants and an emphasis upon social studies in the curriculum. The ideas of 'progressive education' were adopted in varying degrees, and as this implied attention to the whole child, physical education was accorded an important place. The high evaluation of first-hand experience and the enriched curriculum gave recreative activities a new educational importance.

In the boom years of the 1920s, participation in sport and recreation, in spectator interest and support, and in provision for them, grew fast. This resulted in high school and college sport becoming further developed as big business, with inevitable attendant features of athleticism. From 1918 federal and state agencies were co-ordinated by the Commissioner of Education to ensure the provision of health and physical education on a national basis, the increasing numbers of teachers required being trained by the colleges and universities. Expansion of physical education in higher education resulted in the growth of graduate studies, particularly in the evaluation of the effects of exercise, and in the strengthening of professional associations. The content of the work in schools was influenced by the current educational stress upon the need to emphasise social responsibility, the value of direct experience and of a wide range of experience. This led to a decline of formal programmes of training and the development of multi-activity programmes including the rapidly growing popular games.

The 1930s, the years of the Great Depression, brought education cuts and severe restriction on expenditure. The Federal answer was to inaugurate a programme of social reform, reflected in education by concern for the creation of a rational social order. This meant evaluating physical education for its contribution to total education, exemplified by J. F. William's famous dictum that physical education is education *through* the physical rather than *of* the physical. The decade also brought to the fore the concern to educate for leisure, a reflection of the national anxiety for the large numbers of unemployed, and resulting in the growth of departments of recreation in the schools. A general effect was to raise the standards required of teachers, providing a further impetus to the growth of graduate studies in physical education.

In all countries the remarkable growth of sport and recreation in the community encouraged parallel developments in the schools. Official encouragement could be for good or bad reasons. In England it was necessary to justify expenditure on improved facilities and provision, not in educational terms, but in terms of the material benefits to be gained as an investment in preventive medicine or to meet the national need for a physically fit population in a coming war. It was the reassessment of values during wartime that brought a demand for social equity which included an extension of the right to play and of the provision of facilities for play.

Conclusions

Viewed in broad perspective it is evident that the development of physical activities in schools has reflected class divisions in society, and that opportunities for working-class children to play recreative games in schools have been widespread only from the late 1930s. For privileged boys and girls, team games were introduced, became accepted and codified and rose to a pre-eminent position in the public schools for a variety of reasons. Their early development was closely linked with the evolution of boarding education, for they provided a means of occupying boarders in a positive activity which provided healthy exercise, yet also were an antidote to the ill-discipline associated with the unorganised recreations of the early nineteenth century.

Two major influences were discerned in the development of physical education in schools for working-class children before 1870: firstly the sponsoring of physical activities as an ingredient of an instrumentary education, drill providing the physical equivalent of literacy; secondly, the work of those who saw education of and through the physical as an essential part of a wider concept of education.

The application of the Revised Code of 1862 discouraged physical activities, though while propagandists strove to gain official recognition for physical education in the state-aided schools, gymnastics and drill were gaining recognition and spreading in private schools for the children of the middle class and in the public schools. During the period of the school boards, physical drill was regarded as a necessary means of regimenting and disciplining the large numbers of children culled from the streets and brought to school. The disciplinary aim was accentuated by the employment by the various boards of ex-army instructors. However, the most pervasive influence for the development of physical education came from the social reformers, who saw that to ensure the good health of children by feeding and medical care was an essential prerequisite to any form of physical training.

As a direct consequence the major development in physical education in the first quarter of the twentieth century came as the result of the vigorous sponsorship of Swedish therapeutic physical training by the School Medical Service. There was much and varied support for the playing of team games in the elementary schools, reflecting the growth of sport in society, but the lack of playing fields was a major obstacle. The major weaknesses of the education system were half-time schooling and adolescent neglect which dissipated the beneficial results of compulsory education. The Act of 1918 was only partially successful as a remedy. The syllabuses of 1919 and 1933 broadened the base of physical education in the elementary schools, though a wide disparity remained in the provision of facilities and in the standard of work throughout the country. Concern for national security led to a marked revival of official interest in the subject in 1936, but war came too soon for great advances in the provision of necessary facilities to be made.

As part of the reappraisal of society initiated during the war years, the 1944 Education Act was drawn up with plans for ending the socially stigmatised elementary school, which had always afforded little provision for physical education. The major problem of meeting the educational and physical needs of the adolescent generation remained unsolved. The adoption of common standards in the provision of facilities resulted in a major advance in the evolution of the sponsorship of physical education for recreative reasons rather than for therapeutic purposes. The progression from physical drill for disciplinary reasons, to physical exercise for remedial and therapeutic purposes, to recreative activities for broad educational reasons in the fulfilment of the potential of each individual child was made possible. The changing pattern in the schools over 150 years illustrates this advance.

It is evident, too, that this process of evolution was delayed by entrenched attitudes. In the public schools, and the schools which followed their lead, team games retained their premier position because of the value placed on their development of leadership and socially desirable qualities. In the elementary schools too the provision of playing fields and the encouragement of games was for the moral as well as the physical benefits seen to be derived. The physical development of working-class children was in fact given a very low priority until the international crises of the 1930s drew attention to the nation's dependence upon the fitness of the products of these schools. The official sponsoring of a system of therapeutic physical training may have been part of the state's assumption of responsibility for the social welfare of its citizens, but its acceptability was dependent upon its cheapness. The unwillingness to improve physical-education facilities was in accordance with the slow and piecemeal reorganisation of education, with the unwillingness to make the feeding of necessitous children anything but a makeshift and inadequate palliative, with the glossing-over of the true physical state of the children and with the utter neglect of the education of the adolescent. Retention of a naïve belief in the use of physical training to cure fundamental weaknesses due to malnutrition and physical neglect is a remarkable feature.

Also, viewed in large perspective, the period reveals a drawing together of the forms of recreation of the upper and lower classes of society. The spread of the common team games, developed in the public schools as they became predominantly institutions for the education of the sons of the middle classes, to the working classes was made possible by the introduction of shorter hours of work. It was encouraged also by those leaders of society who felt that the benefits to be gained by the inhabitants of industrial communities from participation in sport were important: they saw sport as a highly preferable alternative to other contemporary 'amusements' and 'pastimes', and as one means of improving the quality of life. Shorter working hours and cheap travel encouraged the interest of town dwellers in the countryside. Significantly, the drawing together of social classes during World War I also revealed just how limited was the experience of the working classes in the playing of games, and the interest in sport stimulated during the war years provided an impetus for the post-war expansion of facilities and consequently of the opportunity for play. Economic malaise during the years between the two world wars inhibited government action, so that it was left to charitable organisations to provide sporting facilities to ameliorate the demoralising effect of persistent mass unemployment. Those working-class people who were employed enjoyed a higher standard of living than before. Again, their greater spending power and the advent of the cheap mass-produced motor car brought more people to the countryside. The development of a more democratic view of the provision of opportunities for recreation was reinforced by the concern for the establishment of a more egalitarian society engendered during World War II and put into effect in the social legislation of the post-war period.

Since 1945 there have been many changes in physical education in the schools. In that year the subject ceased to be the direct responsibility of the medical department of the Ministry of Education, and this marks the end of the remedial-therapeutic justification of the work in schools. In the years immediately following the end of World War II the schools imitated the apparatus used for commando and combat training in the armed forces: rope nets, ropes and logs were introduced to primary schools for the children to increase their strength from hanging, climbing and swinging. More sophisticated apparatus was then designed for the same purposes. The growth of national interest in physical recreation is illustrated by the appointment of the first government minister with responsibility for sport in 1963, and in 1965 by the founding of a Sports Council with a special responsibility for aiding sportsmen and women in international competition and for developing a range of facilities for community use. The establishment of facilities to be shared by the adult population and the schools has been a most fruitful outcome of overall planning, which will continue. The period has seen, too, a dramatic increase in outdoor activities, the foundation of the Outward Bound Trust schools being followed by a large number of outdoor-activity centres organised by the local authorities. The Duke of Edinburgh's Award Scheme, launched in 1956, spread interest in outdoor activities throughout youth organisations and schools.

During the 1950s the concepts of movement analysis, applied by Rudolph Laban and Lisa Ullman originally to dance, were used as a means of teaching gymnastics, though many of the men specialist teachers preferred an approach which combined exercises for their anatomical and physiological effects and the direct teaching of skills and agilities. The more general acceptance of physical education as a subject suitable for first-degree work in the 1960s has resulted in a great growth of knowledge of the processes of skill acquisition and a reappraisal of the structure of the subject and its relationship to education as a whole.

During these years protagonists of physical education have based their claims for their subject upon educational arguments, seeking moral, social and psychological benefits in addition to the anatomical and physiological effects. Some of these claims cannot be proved and are viewed sceptically by many teachers of other subjects, and by educational administrators who see little justification for including any broadly based programme of recreative pastimes in school time which would otherwise be allocated to examination subjects. The correspondence columns of professional journals reveal the vexation of many practising teachers of physical education with the involved philosophic statements of the theorists, which apparently have little relevance to the task of teaching boys and girls. Enquiries such as the *Schools Council Enquiry I (1968)* and the *Schools Council Sixth Form Enquiry (1970)* reveal the high regard of both parents and young school-leavers for physical education as a school subject and its continuing importance in school programmes.

There have been advances too in knowledge of the constituents of fitness, and an increasing recognition of the importance of educating young men and women to see fit and sound bodies as a foundation for their present and future health and emotional well-being. In the 1970s there appears to be a growing realisation that because physical education is a process central in the education of children and unique in its effects, it has an inherent strength and dignity which allows it to draw upon the result of work in the human sciences and other academic disciplines, and which justifies this eclecticism.

A comparison of developments in other countries re-emphasises the critical influence of the social and cultural context upon the aims and values of physical education at various times. Nationalism, militarism, elitism, egalitarianism, laissez-faire, social concern, medical therapy and specific educational aims all exert pressures influencing the development of particular kinds of work. Evidently, then, to regard all extensions of facilities and opportunity for physical education and sport as 'good', and all restrictions as 'bad', is to be simplistic.

Physical educationists have frequently been accused of an introverted obsession with aims and objectives, and with the analysis and evaluation of their work in the light of idealistic and pragmatic criteria. Historical study emphasises that this is not merely a desirable process, though often difficult and even painful at times, but essential if physical education is to make its unique and essential contribution to the whole education of the child.

Notes and references

CHAPTER I

1 By 1800 a small number of England's old-established and well-endowed foundations were distinguished as *public* schools, fee-paying schools for the wealthy, as distinct from the *grammar* schools. This separation was confirmed in 1818 when the Charity Commissioners were excused reference to the schools at Westminster, Eton, Winchester, Charterhouse, Harrow and Rugby. To these, Shrewsbury and the two London day schools, St Paul's and Merchant Taylors', were added, to make up the nine investigated by the Public Schools Commission in 1861.

2 Mack, E. C. *Public Schools and British Opinion*, 1 (1930), 40; McIntosh, P. C. *Physical Education in England since 1800* (1952; revised ed 1968), 23.

3 Hans, Nicholas. *New Trends in Education in the Eighteenth Century* (1951), 64–5, 72.

4 Bamford, T. W. *The Rise of the Public Schools* (1967), x.

5 Strachey, Lytton. *Eminent Victorians* (1918), 186.

6 Lamb, G. F. *The Happiest Days* (1959), 230–5.

7 Carleton, J. D. *Westminster School* (1965), 48–9.

8 Lamb, *The Happiest Days*, 223.

9 Carleton, *Westminster*, 55; Bamford, *Public Schools*, 1–5.

10 Musgrove, F. 'Middle-class Education and Employment in the Nineteenth Century', *The Economic History Review*, Second Series 12, no 1 (1959–60), 99ff. The author states that the public schools secured social status for sons whose fathers could not acquire it by wealth alone, but in fact the schools provided a very limited opportunity for the boys to acquire a relative increase in wealth. He also shows that the level of occupational aspiration of Victorian parents for their sons was unrealistic.

11 Strachey, *Eminent Victorians*, 213.

12 Stanley, A. P. *Life of Arnold*, 1 (1844), 29.

13 Armytage, W. H. G. 'Thomas Arnold's Views on Physical Education', *Physical Education*, 47, no 140 (1955), 28.

14 Wymer, N. *Dr Arnold of Rugby* (1953), 142, 174.

15 Arnold, T. *Introductory Lectures in Modern History*, 16–17, quoted in Newsome, D. H. *Godliness and Good Learning* (1961), 1–2. Newsome (ibid 57–8) notes as an example of the application of Arnold's priorities the conversion of W. C. Lake from an athlete neglecting his schoolwork to a scholar who gave up sport.

16 Arnold, T. *Sermons*, 3 (1834), 207–8.

17 Howitt, William. *The Rural Life of England* (1838, 3rd ed 1844), 515–30.

18 'A Layman of the English Church'. *Some Thoughts on the Spread of Mental Culture* (Norwich 1851).

19 Mack, E. C. and Armytage, W. H. G. *Thomas Hughes: The Life of the Author of 'Tom Brown's Schooldays'* (1952), 90.

20 Hollis, C. *Eton, A History* (1960), 243.

21 James, N. G. B. *The History of Mill Hill School* (1908), 155–6.

22 Patterson, W. S. *Sixty Years of Uppingham Cricket* (1909), 3–5.

23 Wainwright, D. *Liverpool Gentlemen* (1960), 72, 274.

24 Parkin, G. R. *The Life and Letters of Edward Thring*, 1 (1910), 76; Patterson, *Uppingham Cricket*, 5, 14.

25 Report of the Public Schools Commission, 1 (1864), 41.

26 Ibid, 2, 147.

27 *Uppingham School Magazine*, 3, no 2 (1865). An editorial reflecting Thring's views.

28 Parkin, *Thring*, 1, 91.

29 Ibid, 118–19.

30 Quotation from Byrne, L. S. R. and Churchill, E. L. *Changing Eton* (1937), 285.

31 Hope Simpson, J. B. *Rugby Since Arnold* (1967), 113–20.

32 Simpson, J. H. *Schoolmaster's Harvest* (1954), 60–3.

33 Firth, J. D'E. *Winchester College* (1949), 43–4, 119–21.

34 Bishop, T. J. M. and Wilkinson, R. *Winchester and the Public School Elite* (1967), 165–8.

35 Wilkinson, R. *The Prefects* (1964), 81ff.

36 Christie, O. F. *A History of Clifton College* (1935), 73–4, 254.

37 Zimmern, A. *The Renaissance of Girls' Education in England* (1898), 153–8.

38 de Zouche, D. E. *Roedean School 1885–1955* (Brighton 1956), 27, 144, 162.

39 Lawrence, P. 'Games and Athletics in Secondary Schools for

Girls', *Special Reports on Educational Subjects*, no 2, 145–52.
40 Hornung, E. W. *Fathers of Men* (1912).
41 Bolitho, Hector. *Alfred Mond, First Lord Melchett* (1933), 45.
42 Grove, W. R. The diaries of a schoolboy at Uppingham 1885–7 (3 vols unpublished), quoted by permission of Miss J. E. Grove.
43 RSIC, VI, 487–8.
44 RSIC, VI, 589–60.
45 Zeigler, Earle F. *Problems in the History and Philosophy of Physical Education and Sport* (New Jersey 1968), 37; Van Dalen, D. B. and Bennett, B. L. *A World History of Physical Education* (New Jersey 1953; 2nd ed 1971), 394.
46 See Jackson, Myles, 'College Football Has Become a Losing Business', in Loy, J. W., Jr and Kenyon, G. S. *Sport, Culture and Society* (New York 1969), for the growth and extent of the business of intercollegiate football. The phrase quoted occurs in Dulles, F. R. *America Learns to Play* (New York 1940), 350.
47 Newsome, *Godliness and Good Learning*, 238.
48 Tennyson, Sir Charles. 'They Taught the World to Play', *Victorian Studies*, 2, no 3 (March 1959), 222.

CHAPTER 2

1 Arnold, *Sermons*, 3, 207.
2 Kingsley, Charles. *Health and Education* (1874), 86.
3 Hughes, Thomas. *Tom Brown's Schooldays* (1857), 164.
4 Briggs, Asa. 'Thomas Hughes and the Public Schools', *Victorian People* (New York 1955), 143–9.
5 Stephen, Leslie. *Sketches from Cambridge* (1865), 81.
6 Rothblatt, Sheldon. *The Revolution of the Dons* (1968), 189.
7 Newsome, *Godliness and Good Learning*, 216.
8 Briggs, *Thomas Hughes*, 146.
9 Beales, D. 'An International Crisis. The Italian Question in 1859', in Appleman, P., Madden, W. A. and Wolff, M., *1859: Entering an Age of Crisis* (Indiana 1959), 192–3.
10 Fletcher, C. R. L. *Edmund Warre* (1922), 97–102.
11 Semmel, B. *Imperialism and Social Reform* (1960), *passim*.
12 Rowse, A. L. *The English Spirit* (1966), 229.
13 *Greshamian*, 3, no 7 (1909), 87.
14 *Uppingham School Magazine*, no 52, 298–9.
15 See Wakeford, J. *The Cloistered Elite* (1969), 38ff for a discussion of boarding schools in terms of Goffman's concept of a 'total institution'.

16 See Wilkinson, R. H. 'The Gentleman Ideal and the Maintenance of a Political Elite', in Musgrave, P. W. (ed), *Sociology, History and Education* (1970), 126–42.

17 Baron, G. 'Some Aspects of the Headmaster Tradition', in Musgrave, *Sociology, History and Education*, 187.

18 Hope Simpson, J. B. *Rugby since Arnold* (1967), 223.

19 Collins, Tom. *School and Sport* (1905), 38ff.

20 *Uppingham School Magazine*, no 26, 257–8.

21 Parkin, *Thring*, 1, 238.

22 Ogilvie, V. *The English Public Schools* (1957), 165.

23 *Uppingham School Magazine*, no 1, 41–2.

CHAPTER 3

1 Firth, J. D'E. *Winchester College* (1949), 139.

2 Grove, *Diaries*.

3 Sandford, E. G. *Memoirs of Archbishop Temple*, 1 (1906), 212.

4 James, *Mill Hill*, 218, 252–62.

5 Mack, *Public Schools*, 2, 155.

6 Anon. *Sanderson of Oundle* (1923), note on 28.

7 See Smith, W. David. 'A Study of Physical Education in the Schools . . .' (MPhil thesis, University of East Anglia, 1971), Appendix 1.

8 Pattison, Mark. *Suggestions on Academical Organisation* (Edinburgh 1868), 316.

9 Lyttelton, E. 'Athletics in Public Schools', *Nineteenth Century* (January 1880), 46–55.

10 Lunn, A. *The Harrovians* (1913), 34, 44ff. Lunn shows how the effect of the established ethos and the attitudes of boys in authority created for individual boys a sense of boredom, frustration and futility.

11 Gray, H. B. *The Public Schools and the Empire* (1913), 188. Gray, the headmaster of Bradfield, discusses the reasons for the adulation of games, attacks exaggerated notions and indicts the construction of outlook that follows conformity. He wishes to see a more realistic preparation for service to the empire.

12 Ford, L. 'Public School Athletics', in Cookson, C. (ed), *Essays on Secondary Education* (1898), 294.

13 Montague, C. E. *Rough Justice* (1926), 130–2. This is one of a number of novels which attack the values implicit in public-school education.

14 Collins, W. *Man and Wife* (1870), in 3 vols. Collins appears to have

had little effect in his attempt to curb the growth of athleticism, for there is no evidence of support for his attack. He wrote angrily of athleticism as a 'revival of barbarism', citing the riot at the Oxford Commemoration of 1869 and the sacking of Christchurch library as results.

15 For example, Worsley, T. C. *Barbarians and Philistines* (1940), 107. In this work Worsley challenges the most cherished estimates of the value of the boarding education of public schools, including its suitability as the initial training of army officers. He concludes that this is an education suitable for the mid-adolescent period only, that its total effect is to barbarise and that it results in arrested development. Similar charges are repeated in *Flannelled Fool*, an autobiographical work published in 1967.

16 Faber, G. *Jowett, a Portrait with a Background* (1957), 65, 84–5.

17 Lyttelton, G. W. 'Athletics', *The Public Schools from Within* (1880), 192.

18 Annan, N. *Roxburgh of Stowe* (1965), 11.

19 Kipling, R. 'The Islanders', *The Five Nations* (1949), 128.

20 Browne, M. *A Dream of Youth* (1918), 54–8.

21 Murray, G. W., of Marlborough College, has provided in a personal communication (1970) much of the information used here about developments in the schools as the result of army connections.

22 See McIntosh, *Physical Education*, 156ff for a full account.

23 Hope Simpson, *Rugby*, 171.

24 See Eager, W. McG. *Making Men* (1953), 103–11.

25 Gibbon, F. P. *William Smith of the Boys Brigade* (1934), 65–9.

26 Reynolds, E. E. *The Scout Movement* (1950), 71.

27 Saunders, H. St G. *The Left Handshake* (1949), 51, 96. During the air raids 1939–45 194 Scouts were killed on duty.

28 Campbell Stewart, W. A. *The Educational Innovators*, 2, 1881–1967 (1968), 37.

29 Campbell Stewart, W. A. *Quakers and Education* (1953), 157–9.

30 Carpenter, P. in 'The Outward Bound Schools: A Means for the Development and Assessment of Character' (BLitt thesis, Oxford 1958) evaluates the methods and results of Hahn's work as applied in the Outward Bound Schools. The Duke of Edinburgh's Award Scheme, established in 1956, applies Hahn's theories to the training of members of youth organisations and others. Carpenter, P. 'The Award Scheme Reviewed', *The Cambridge Institute of Education Bulletin*, 3, no 12 (1970), assesses the impact and influences of the scheme in its fourteen years' existence.

31 The crucial problem is to find acceptable methods of evaluating character. Drinkwater, D. J. in 'An Assessment of the Value of Physical Education in Character Training for Boys' (MA(Ed) thesis, London 1956), concludes from his work that in the field of education physical education has no significant value as a determinant of social actions beyond the immediate environment. In contrast, Carpenter's researches and the work of Fletcher, B. *The Challenge of Outward Bound* (1971), illustrate the conviction of participants and their sponsors of the value of Outward Bound courses in developing desirable character traits.

32 Dukes, C. *Health at School* (4th ed 1905) and Horsfall, T. C. *Proceedings of the Conference on Education under Health Conditions* (1885), 203–4, 225.

33 See Myers, C. S. *Industrial Psychology in Great Britain* (1933).

34 McIntosh, *Physical Education*, 213ff, contains details of these developments.

35 May, J. *Madam Bergman-Österberg* (1969), contains a detailed account of the extent of her influence.

36 Murray, G. W. 'Physical Education in the Curriculum', in Laborde, E. D. (ed), *Problems in Modern Education* (1938).

37 Jacks, L. P. 'The Wider Possibilities of Physical Culture', in Laborde, E. D., *Education of Today* (Cambridge 1935), 44–5, 49–51.

CHAPTER 4

1 Edgworth, R. L. *Memoirs*, 1 (1820), 268.

2 Recently published works include Simon, B. *Studies in the History of Education 1780–1870* (1960), 193–7; Campbell Stewart, W. A. and McCann, W. P. *The Educational Innovators* (1967), 53–74; Silver, H. *Robert Owen on Education* (1969).

3 Silver, *Robert Owen*, 163.

4 Podmore, F. *Robert Owen* (1906), 144–5.

5 Silver, *Robert Owen*, 164.

6 Pollard, H. M. *Pioneers of Popular Education* (1956), 141.

7 Raymont, T. *A History of the Education of Young Children* (1956), 151.

8 Wilderspin, S. *The Infant System* (1852), 101–7.

9 Sanderson, Michael. 'The Basic Education of Labour in Lancashire 1780–1839' (PhD thesis, Cambridge 1966), 337–41.

10 Campbell Stewart and McCann, *Innovators*, 74ff.

11 Simon, *History of Education*, 258–69, contains an account of Lovett as an educationist.

12 Dixon *et alia, Landmarks,* section 6 describes these developments.
13 Pollard, *Pioneers,* has brief accounts of these schools.
14 Pestalozzi, J. H. *How Gertrude Teaches Her Children* (1907 ed), 177–8.
15 Campbell Stewart and McCann, *Innovators,* 172–6.
16 Southery, R. *The Life of the Revd Andrew Bell,* 3 (1844), 89.
17 Pollard, *Pioneers,* 146ff.
18 Adkins, T. *The History of St John's College, Battersea* (1906), 57–8.
19 McIntosh, *Physical Education,* has a detailed account of this.
20 Hill, M. D. *Public Education* (1835), 133–5.
21 Pritchard, F. C. *Methodist Secondary Education* (1949), 135–41.
22 Felkin, F. W. *From Gower St to Frognal* (1909), 12.
23 *Minutes of the Committee of Council on Education 1839–40,* 71.
24 Ibid, 16ff.
25 Leese, J. *Personalities and Power in English Education* (1950), 116.
26 McNair, D. 'The Development of Physical Education in Scotland before 1914' (MEd thesis, Manchester 1961), 35ff, shows the development of ideas from Owen to Wilderspin and Stow.
27 Stow, D. *The Training System* (1845 ed), 54.
28 Adamson, J. W. *English Education 1789–1902* (1964), 136ff.
29 Pritchard, *Methodist Education,* 135–41.
30 *Report of the Assistant Commissioners . . .,* 2 (1861), 98.
31 House of Commons, 168, 22.
32 Leese, *Personalities and Power,* 118–19.
33 Quoted in Adamson, *English Education,* 300.
34 McIntosh, *Physical Education,* 101.
35 More details of continental developments can be found in the relevant sections of Dixon *et alia, Landmarks;* and Van Dalen, D. B. and Bennett, B. L. *A World History of Physical Education* (2nd ed New Jersey 1971).
36 Gerber, E. W. *Innovators and Institutions in Physical Education* (Philadelphia 1971), 276–82.
37 Redmond, G. 'The Caledonian Games and American Track and Field in the 19th Century', *Bulletin of Physical Education,* 9, no 1 (1972), 15–22.

CHAPTER 5

1 Mackenzie, W. L. *The Health of the School Child* (1906), 51.
2 Quoted in Mackintosh, J. M. *Trends of Opinion about the Public Health 1901–51* (1953), 29.
3 Gorst, *Children of the Nation,* 52.

4   A large number of these were indeed provided by the societies, especially the National Society, in response to the challenge of the boards. See Dent, M. C. *1870–1970 Century of Growth in English Education* (1970), 13–15, for details of expansion.

5   Sadler, M. E. and Edwards, J. W. in *Special Reports on Educational Subjects*, no 1 (1897), 67, state that in 1872 there were 926 such schools and by 1895 there were 1,572—a small proportion of the total number of schools.

6   Spencer, F. H. *An Inspector's Testament* (1938), 64–5.

7   Horsfall, T. C. (ed). *Proceedings of the Conference on Education under Healthy Conditions* (1885), 214ff.

8   *Report of the Royal Commission on Physical Training (Scotland* 1), (1903), 290, 337.

9   Ibid, 156 and Spalding, T. A. and Canney, T. S. A. *The Work of the London School Board* (1900), 237ff.

10 Molyneaux, D. D. 'The Development of Physical Recreation in the Birmingham District from 1871–92' (MA thesis, Birmingham 1957), 217ff, contains a full account of the work in schools in this area.

11 *Special Reports*, 2 (1898), 40.

12 Spencer, *Testament*, 65.

13 Philpott, H. B. *London at School* (1904), 119.

14 Ibid, 308.

15 Quoted in Webb, Beatrice. *My Apprenticeship* (1950 ed), 119.

16 There was strong opposition from ratepayers to this appointment —see May, J. *Madame Bergman-Österberg* (1969). The Earl of Meath refers to a grant of £300 from the Metropolitan Gardens Association to the board to pay for 'bringing over physical exercises teachers from Sweden', *RCPT (Scotland)*, 2, 339.

17 May, *Bergman-Österberg*, 24.

18 Maclure, J. S. *Educational Documents, England and Wales 1816–1967* (1968), 130.

19 Sellman, R. R. *Devon Village Schools in the Nineteenth Century* (1967), 139.

20 Pepler, H. D. C., in Laurie, A. D. (ed), *The Teacher's Encyclopaedia* 4 (1911), 175ff.

21 Booth, C. *Poverty*, 3 (1902), 207.

22 *RI-DCPD*, 2 (1904), 455.

23 The leading protagonists of free meals on the London School Board were Annie Besant and Stewart Headlam; see Simon, B. *Education and the Labour Movement 1870–1920* (1965), 156.

24 See Lowndes, G. A. N. *Margaret McMillan* (1960), 52ff.
25 This has been claimed to be the first appointment of its kind, though Dr W. R. Smith was appointed by the London School Board in 1890—see Newman, Sir G. *The Building of a Nation's Health* (1939), 187.
26 See Mackintosh, *Opinions about the Public Health*, 24-6, for the ineffectiveness of the officials of the Local Government Board as an example of officialdom inhibiting progress.
27 Lowndes, *Margaret McMillan*, 95.
28 Kekewich, Sir G. *The Education Department and After* (1920), 56.
29 Leese, J. *Personalities and Power in English Education* (1950), 179.
30 In this view they had a supporter of the opposite political persuasion in Sir John Gorst.
31 Martin, J. W. 'State Education at Home and Abroad', *Fabian Tract no 52* (1894), 13.
32 Philpott, *London at School*, 122ff.
33 *Special Reports*, no 2, 160-1.
34 Lowndes, G. A. N. *The Silent Social Revolution* (2nd ed 1969), 27.
35 Mackintosh, *Opinions about the Public Health*, 8.
36 For details of developments see relevant sections of Dixon *et alia*. *Landmarks*; and van Dalen and Bennett, *World History of Physical Education*.
37 Quoted in Samuel, R. H. and Hinton, Thomas R. *Education and Society in Modern Germany* (1949), 155.
38 Ibid, 156-7.
39 van Dalen and Bennett, *World History of Physical Education*, 394.
40 Curti, Merle. *The Social Ideas of American Educators* (New York 1935), 246-7.
41 Cremin, L. A. *The Transformation of the School* (New York 1962), 62ff.
42 van Dalen and Bennett, *World History*, 404.
43 Ibid, 427.

CHAPTER 6

1 Maurice, Sir F. 'Where to Get Men', *The Contemporary Review* (1902), 62, and 'National Health: A Soldier's Study', *The Contemporary Review* (1903), 83.
2 Schedule 3 (Day Code 1901) in *Educational Reports* (1901), 20, 143.
3 *Schoolmaster* 62 (October 1902), 529-30.
4 *Report of the Inter-Departmental Committee on the Model Course of Physical Exercises 1904 (Cd 2032)*, 3.

5 Circular 515 which accompanied the syllabus emphasised the freedom of teachers to develop a 'considerable variety' in the work.

6 Mackenzie, *Health of the School Child*, 52. Mackenzie records that he and Professor Hay were 'freely accused of gross exaggeration', indicating just how unpalatable their findings and the decisions based upon them were.

7 See Simon, *Education and the Labour Movement*, 133–5, 156ff.

8 Mackintosh, *Public Health*, 31.

9 Gorst, *Children of the Nation*, 1.

10 Quoted in Newman, Sir George. *The Building of a Nation's Health* (1939), 458–9.

11 Report of the Chief Medical Officer (1908), 86.

12 Ibid, 44–5.

13 RCMO (1909), 28–30.

14 Report of the Norwich School Medical Officer (1911).

15 RCMO (1909), 109–80.

16 Ibid, 175.

17 Quoted in Webb, I. M. 'Women's Physical Education in Great Britain 1800–1966 . . .' (MEd Thesis, Leicester 1967), 305.

18 Spalding, M. H. 'The Case for the Swedish System', in Adams, J., *The New Teaching* (1918), 378.

19 Woodward, A. C. 'The Development of Physical Education in Schools in England and Wales, 1907 to 1933 . . .' (MEd thesis, Manchester 1968), 90.

20 Roper, R. E. *Organised Play at Home and Abroad* (1911), *passim*.

21 HC, 39, 1500.

22 HL, 22, 677–8.

23 Report of the Board of Education (1914–15), 18ff and Report of the Board of Education (1915–16), 1 and 13.

24 See Simon, *Education and the Labour Movement*, 351.

25 Bray, R. *Boy Labour and Apprenticeship* (1911), 106–9.

26 Freeman, A. *Boy Life and Labour* (1914), 87–9, 168–72.

27 Ibid, 187.

28 HC, 87, 799–852.

29 RCMO (1917), 21.

30 Hearnshaw, L. S. *A Short History of British Psychology* (1964), 257; and Bramwell, R. D. *Elementary School Work 1900–1925* (Durham 1961), *passim*.

31 Samuel and Thomas, *Modern Germany*, 20.

32 Curti, *Social Ideas*, 248.

33 See van Dalen and Bennett, *World History*, 433–7.
34 See Butts, R. F. and Cremin, L. A. *A History of Education in American Culture* (New York 1953), 404–16.

CHAPTER 7

1 See Bruce, M. *The Coming of the Welfare State* (1968), 234ff, for a consideration of what he terms 'The Two Englands'.
2 See Bernbaum, G. *Social Change and the Schools 1918–1944* (1967), 30ff.
3 Myers, C. S. *Industrial Psychology in Great Britain* (1933), 16–17, 44ff.
4 Keith, Sir A. 'Six Lectures on Man's Posture: Its Evolution and Disorder', *British Medical Journal* (1923).
5 RCMO (1935), 44.
6 RBE (1922–3). There were forty-seven men at the Sheffield course and twenty women at Reading in 1921–2.
7 RCMO (1934), 37ff.
8 Ibid, 138.
9 RCMO (1939–45), 35ff. See *Our Towns*, a study made in 1939–42 by the Women's Group of Public Welfare, for a detailed account of evacuated children. This study shows (67ff) that the statistics of 'uncleanliness' based upon routine medical inspection are of no value as a guide, inspections by school nurses revealing a much higher incidence of infection. Dr K. Mellanby's investigations showed an infestation rate of 30 per cent among boys, and 50 per cent among girls, of school age: this was approximately three times as high as the School Medical Officers' estimates.
10 Lowndes, *Silent Social Revolution*, 171–2.
11 M'Gonigle, G. C. M. and Kirby, J. *Poverty and Public Health* (1936), 52–3.
12 Boyd Orr, J. *Food, Health and Income* (1936), *passim*.
13 M'Gonigle and Kirby, *Poverty and Public Health*, 53–4, 141ff. The terms 'malnutrition' and 'subnormal nutrition' were ambiguous. Attempts to provide objective criteria of assessment were not successful. The CMO felt there was no better means of assessment than the subjective estimate of the school doctor. The basic difficulty was that any means of evaluation which would have resulted in a large increase in recommendation for free meals would not have been accepted politically.
14 RCMO (1920), 146–9.

15 RCMO (1926), 137. See Leff, S. and Leff, V. *The School Health Service* (1959), 78–87 for details.
16 HC, 320, 112.
17 Eager, W. McG. and Secretan, H. A. *Unemployment among Boys* (1925), 17.
18 Eager, *Making Men*, 412ff.
19 Trevelyan, G. M. in Coburn, D. *Youth Hostel Story* (1950), 1–2.
20 HC, 320, 105.
21 RBE (1938–9), 47ff.
22 RCMO (1937), 37.
23 RCMO (1938), 28.
24 HC, 320, 78–82.
25 HC, 320, 114ff.
26 HC, 322, 252–6.
27 McIntosh, *Physical Education*, 244, from *Civil Appropriation Accounts 1937–9*.
28 Mess, H. A. and others. *Voluntary Social Services since 1918* (1947), 136.
29 RCMO (1939–45), 37ff.
30 Lynch, G. W. in *The Times Educational Supplement* (26 June 1970).
31 RCMO (1939–45), 7ff.
32 Bruce, *Welfare State*, 236.
33 See Lowndes, *Silent Social Revolution*, Chapter 13.
34 RCMO (1939–45), 36–7.
35 Lowndes, *Silent Social Revolution*, 221.
36 *Regulations Prescribing Standards for School Premises* (HMSO) 1944.
37 Mackintosh, *Public Health*, 108.
38 Spencer, *Inspector's Testament*, 310.
39 Grunberger, R. *A Social History of the Third Reich* (1971), 285ff.

Bibliography

It is inappropriate here to list fully the manuscripts, pamphlets and printed sources consulted. Such a list is included in the bibliography of my thesis, the title of which is included in section 3 below.

I OFFICIAL PAPERS

Minutes of the Committee of Council on Education, 1839–40

Report of the Commissioners appointed to inquire into the state of Popular Education in England (Newcastle Commission), 1861

Report of the Public Schools Commission (Clarendon Commission), 1864

Report of the Schools Inquiry Commission (Taunton Commission), 1868

Report of the Commission appointed to inquire into the Elementary Education Acts (Cross Commission), 1888

Special Reports on Educational Subjects, Vol I, 1896–7; Vol II, 1898

Board of Education, *Day School Code*, 1901

Board of Education, *Model Course of Physical Training*, 1902

Report of the Royal Commission on Physical Training (Scotland), 1903

Report of the Inter-Departmental Committee on Physical Deterioration, 1904

Report of the Inter-Departmental Committee on the Model Course of Physical Exercises, 1904

Board of Education, *Circular 515*, 22 August 1904

Board of Education, *Syllabus of Physical Exercises*, 1904
Board of Education, *Handbook of Suggestions for Teachers*, 1905
Report on Underfed Children at Elementary Schools, 1905
Board of Education, *Syllabus of Physical Exercises for Schools*, 1909
Report of the Departmental Committee appointed to inquire into
    Certain Questions in connection with the Playgrounds of
    Public Elementary Schools, 1912
Board of Education, *Syllabus of Physical Training for Schools*, 1919
The Education of the Adolescent (Hadow Report), 1926
Report on the Primary School (Hadow Report), 1931
Board of Education, *Syllabus of Physical Training for Schools*, 1933
Board of Education, *Circular 1445*, 1936
White Paper on Physical Training and Recreation Act, 1937
Report on Secondary (Grammar and Technical) Education (Spens
    Report), 1938
White Paper on Educational Reconstruction, 1943

In addition
Reports of the Board of Education from 1900–1 to 1938–9 and
    1947
Reports of the Chief Medical Officer from 1908 to 1956 and 1957
Hansard, reports of debates in the House of Commons and House
    of Lords

2 SELECTED SECONDARY SOURCES

The place of publication is London, unless otherwise stated

Adamson, J. W.	*English Education 1789–1902* (1964)
Annan, N. G.	*Leslie Stephen. His Thought and Character in Relation to his Time* (1951)
	Roxburgh of Stowe (1965)
Anon	*Sanderson of Oundle* (1923)
Archer, R. J.	*Secondary Education in the Nineteenth Century* (Cambridge 1921)
Bamford, T. W.	*The Rise of the Public Schools* (1967)
	Thomas Arnold (1960)

Baron, G.   *Society, Schools and Progress* (1965)
                     'Some Aspects of the "Headmaster Tradi-
                     tion"', in Musgrave, P. W. (ed) *Sociology,
                     History and Education* (1970)
Beales, D.   'An International Crisis. The Italian Ques-
                     tion in 1859', in Appleman, P., Madden,
                     W. A. and Wolff, M. (ed) *1859: Entering
                     an Age of Crisis* (Indiana 1959)
Benson, A. C.   *The Schoolmaster* (1908)
                     The Upton Letters (1906)
Bernbaum, G.   *Social Change and the Schools 1918–44* (1967)
Bishop, T. J. M. and *Winchester and the Public School Elite* (1967)
  Wilkinson, R.
Bramwell, R. D.   *Elementary School Work 1900–25* (Durham
                     1961)
Bray, R. A.   *Boy Labour and Apprenticeship* (1911)
                     The Town Child (1907)
Briggs, Asa   *Victorian People* (New York 1955)
Browne, M.   *A Dream of Youth* (1918)
Bruce, M.   *The Coming of the Welfare State* (1968)
Butts, R. F.,   *A History of Education in American Culture*
  Freeman, R. and   (New York 1953)
  Cremin, L. A.
Carleton, J. D.   *Westminster School* (1965)
Christie, O. F.   *A History of Clifton College* (1935)
Clarke, A. K.   *A History of Cheltenham Ladies College*
                     (1953)
Coburn, O.   *Youth Hostel Story* (1950)
Cohen, E. W.   *English Social Services* (1949)
Collins, L. B.   *Physical Education in the Secondary School*
  Kozman, H. C. and   (New York 1940)
  Stolz, H. R.
Collins, T.   *School and Sport* (1905)
Cremin, L. A.   *The Transformation of the School* (New York
                     1962)

Curti, M.	*The Social Ideas of American Educators* (New York 1935)
David, A. A.	*Life and the Public Schools* (1932)
Dent, H. C.	*Education in Transition* (1944)
	1870–1970 Century of Growth in English Education (1970)
Dilke, C.	*Dr Moberly's Mint-Mark* (1965)
Dobbs, A. E.	*Education and Social Movement* (1919)
Draper, F. W. M.	*Four Centuries of Merchant Taylors Schools* (1962)
Dukes, C.	*Health at School* (1905)
Dulles, F. R.	*America Learns to Play* (New York 1940)
Eager, W. McG.	*Making Men* (1953)
Eager, W. McG. and Secretan, H. A.	*Unemployment Among Boys* (1925)
Firth J. D'E.	*Winchester College* (1949)
Fletcher, B.	*The Challenge of Outward Bound* (1971)
Freeman, A.	*Boy Life and Labour* (1914)
Friend, G. E.	*The Schoolboy. A Study of His Nutrition, Physical Development and Health* (Cambridge 1935)
Gerber, E. W.	*Innovators and Institutions in Physical Education* (Philadelphia 1971)
Gibbon, F. P.	*William A. Smith of the Boys Brigade* (1934)
Good, H. G.	*A History of American Education* (New York 2nd ed 1962)
Gorst, Sir J.	*The Children of the Nation* (1906)
Gourlay, A. B.	*A History of Sherborne School* (Winchester 1951)
Graves, J.	*Policy and Progress in Secondary Education* (1943)
Graves, R.	*Goodbye to All That* (1929)
Gray, H. B.	*The Public Schools and the Empire* (1913)
Griffin, F. W. W.	*The Scientific Basis of Physical Education* (1937)

Griffin F. W. W. and McConnel, J. K.	*Health and Muscular Habits* (1937)
Grunberger, R.	*A Social History of the Third Reich* (1971)
Hammond, J. L. and B.	*The Bleak Age* (1934)
Hans, N.	*New Trends in Education in the Eighteenth Century* (1951)
Hedley, G. W. and Murray, G. W.	*Physical Education for Boys* (1936)
Hogan, J.	*Impelled into Experience* (1969)
Howitt, W.	*The Rural Life of England* (3rd ed 1844)
Hughes, T.	*Tom Brown's Schooldays* (1857)
	Tom Brown at Oxford (1862)
Jacks, L. P.	*Education Through Recreation* (1932)
	'Physical Illiteracy', in Boyd, W. (ed) *The Challenge of Leisure* (1936)
	'The Wider Possibilities of Physical Culture', in Laborde, E. D. (ed) *Education of Today* (Cambridge 1935)
Jacks, M. L.	*Education as a Social Factor* (1937)
	Physical Education (1938)
James, D.	*Outward Bound* (1957)
James, N. G. B.	*The History of Mill Hill School 1807–1907* (1908)
Kamm, J.	*How Different from Us* (1958)
Katz, M. B.	*The Irony of Early School Reform* (Cambridge, Mass 1968)
Kekewich, Sir G. W.	*The Education Department and After* (1920)
Knudsen, K. A.	*Textbook of Gymnastics 1 and 2* (1947 ed)
Lamb, G. F.	*The Happiest Days* (1959)
Laurie A. P. (ed)	*The Teacher's Encyclopaedia* (1911)
Leese, J.	*Personalities and Power in English Education* (1950)
Leff, S.	*The Health of the People* (1950)
Leff, S. and Leff, V.	*The School Health Service* (1959)

Lowndes, G. A. N.   *Margaret McMillan* (1960)
                     The Silent Social Revolution 1895–1965 (1969)
Loy, J. W. (jr) and *Sport, Culture and Society* (New York 1969)
Kenyon G. S.
Lunn, A.   *The Harrovians* (1913)
M'Gonigle, G. C. M. *Poverty and Public Health* (1936)
and Kirby, J.
Mack, E. C.   *Public Schools and British Opinion 1. 1790–
                     1860* (1930)
                     *Public Schools and British Opinion 2. since
                     1860* (New York 1941)
Mack, E. C. and   *Thomas Hughes. The Life of the Author of
Armytage, W. H. G.   'Tom Brown's Schooldays'* (1952)
MacKenzie, R. L.   *Almond of Loretto* (1905)
Mackenzie, W. L.   *The Health of the School Child* (1906)
Mackintosh, J. M.   *Trends of Opinion about the Public Health
                     1901–51* (1953)
McIntosh, P. C.   *Physical Education since 1800* (revised ed
                     1968)
                     Sport in Society (1963)
McIntosh, P. C.,   *Landmarks in the History of Physical Educa-
Dixon, J. G.   tion* (1957)
Munrow, A. D. and
Willetts, R. F.
Maclure, J. S.   *Educational Documents, England and Wales
                     1816–1967* (1968)
Martin, R. B.   *The Dust of Combat* (1959)
May, J.   *Madame Bergman-Österberg* (1969)
Montague, C. E.   *Rough Justice* (1926)
Murray, G. W. and   *Physical Education and Health* (1966)
Hunter, T. A. A.
Musgrove, F.   'Middle Class Families and Schools 1780–
                     1880', in Musgrave, P. W. (ed) *Sociology,
                     History and Education* (1970)
Newman, Sir G.   *The Building of a Nation's Health* (1939)

Newsome, D.   *Godliness and Good Learning* (1961)
                     A History of Wellington College 1859–1959
                     (1959)
Orr, J. Boyd   *Food, Health and Income* (1936)
Women's Group on   *Our Towns* (Oxford 1943)
Public Welfare
Parkin, G. R.   *The Life and Letters of Edward Thring* (2 vols
                     1910)
Paterson, A. and   *Background Readings for Physical Education*
Hallberg, E. C.   (New York 1967)
Philpott, H. B.   *London at School* (1904)
Roper, R. E.   *Movement and Thought* (1938)
                     Organised Play at Home and Abroad (1911)
                     Physical Education in Relation to School Life
                     (1917)
Samuel, R. H. and   *Education and Society in Modern Germany*
Thomas, R. H.   (1949)
Selleck, R. J. W.   *The New Education 1870–1914* (1968)
Semmel, B.   *Imperialism and Social Reform* (1960)
Silver, H.   *The Concept of Popular Education* (1965)
Simon, B.   *Education and the Labour Movement 1870–
                     1920* (1965)
                     Studies in the History of Education 1780–1870
                     (1960)
Spencer, F. H.   *An Inspector's Testament* (1938)
Stanley, A. P.   *The Life and Correspondence of Thomas Arnold*
                     (2 vols 1844)
Stewart, W. A.   *The Educational Innovators 1881–1967* (1968)
Campbell
Stewart, W. A.   *The Educational Innovators 1750–1880* (1967)
Campbell and
McCann, W. P.
Stow, D.   *The Training System* (1845)
Strutt, J.   *The Sports and Pastimes of the People of Eng-
                     land* (1801)

Sturt, M.	*The Education of the People* (1967)
Tropp, A.	*The School Teachers* (1957)
Van Dalen, D. B. and Bennett, B. L.	*A World History of Physical Education* (2nd ed, New Jersey 1971)
Wakeford, J.	*The Cloistered Elite* (1969)
Waugh, A.	*The Loom of Youth* (1964)
Weinberg, I.	*The English Public Schools* (1967)
Wilderspin, S.	*Early Discipline Illustrated* (1832)
	The Infant System (1852)
Wilkinson, R.	*Governing Elites* (New York 1969)
	The Prefects (1964)
Williams, J. F.	*The Principles of Physical Education* (Philadelphia, 5th ed 1948)
Worsley, T. C.	*Barbarians and Philistines* (1940)
	Flannelled Fool (1967)
Zeigler, E. F.	*Problems in the History and Philosophy of Physical Education and Sport* (New Jersey 1968)
Zimmern, A.	*The Renaissance of Girls' Education in England* (1898)
de Zouche, D. E.	*Roedean School 1855-1955* (Brighton 1955)

3   UNPUBLISHED THESES

Carpenter, P.	'The Outward Bound Schools: A Means for the Development and Assessment of Character' (BLitt Oxford 1958)
Drinkwater, D. J.	'An Assessment of the Value of Physical Education in Character Training for Boys' (MA(Ed) London 1956)
McNair, D.	'The Development of Physical Education in Scotland before 1914' (MEd Manchester 1961)
Molyneaux, D. D.	'The Development of Physical Recreation in the Birmingham District from 1871-1892' (MA Birmingham 1957)

Smith, W. D. 'A Study of the Provision of Physical Education in the Schools in the Nineteenth and Twentieth Centuries: An examination of Changing Views' (MPhil East Anglia 1971)

Webb, I. M. 'Women's Physical Education in Great Britain 1800–1966, with special reference to Teacher Training' (MEd Leicester 1967)

Woodward, A. C. 'The Development of Physical Education in England as shown in the Parliamentary Debates and the National Press during the period 1870–1918' (Diploma in Advanced Study in Education, Manchester 1964)

'The Development of Physical Education in Schools in England and Wales 1907–33' (MEd Manchester 1968)

Acknowledgements

I have to thank many people who directly or indirectly made this work possible. The governors of Keswick Hall College of Education and the principal, the Reverend Canon John Gibbs, granted me study-leave to prepare the thesis upon which this book is based. Dr Charles Harrison and Dr Lincoln Ralphs made available records and documents pertaining to schools in Norwich and Norfolk. The headmasters of the schools selected for special study, S. M. Andrews, W. A. Barker, A. L. Creed, L. Bruce Lockhart, W. S. Porter and John Royds, allowed the use of documents and provided generous hospitality.

Professor P. A. Smithells of the University of Otago and G. W. Murray of Marlborough College gave most generously of their time to write memoranda of their work in the 1930s. Miss J. E. Grove kindly let me read her father's diaries. Mrs Hilda Elliston typed the draft with customary accuracy and an unfailing cheerfulness.

Dr Michael Sanderson of the University of East Anglia read the whole text and made many valuable suggestions and comments. My chief debt is owed to my former tutor, Professor Roy Campbell of the University of Stirling. He merits gratitude commensurate with his boundless encouragement. Responsibility for any errors of fact, analysis or judgement that remain is mine.

W. D. S.

Index

Page numbers in italic refer to principal entries for that subject; for Acts of Parliament see under that heading; for Committees and Commissions see under Reports